HEIDI ANNE MESME

BIG
WORDS
FOR YOUNG READERS

Teaching Kids in Grades K to 5 to Decode—and Understand—Words With Multiple Syllables and Morphemes

SCHOLASTIC

DEDICATION

*For my husband, Eric, who has tolerated and loved me patiently
across decades, and who shares my passion for improving the lives of kids.*

Senior Vice President and Publisher: Tara Welty
Editorial Director: Sarah Longhi
Development Editor: Raymond Coutu
Production Editor: Danny Miller
Assistant Editor: Samantha Unger
Creative Director: Tannaz Fassihi
Interior Designer: Maria Lilja

Photos ©: 15: GoodLifeStudio/Getty Images; 31: SolStock/Getty Images; 32: SolStock/Getty Images; 49: chuanchai/Getty Images; 86: kali9/Getty Images. All other photos © Shutterstock.com. All icons created by The Noun Project.

Credits: 21: "The Reading Rope" from "Connecting Early Language and Literacy to Later Reading (Dis)Abilities: Evidence, Theory, and Practice" by H. S. Scarborough. Originally published in *Handbook of Early Literacy Research*, Volume 1. Copyright © 2001 by Guilford Press. Reprinted by permission of Guilford Press; 22: "The Active View of Reading" from "The Science of Reading Progresses: Communicating Advances Beyond the Simple View of Reading" by Nell K. Duke and Kelly B. Cartwright. Originally published in *Reading Research Quarterly*, Volume 56. Copyright © 2021 by the Authors. Reprinted by permission of John Wiley & Sons, Inc.; 136: Morpheme Triangles adapted from "Interactive Frames for Vocabulary Growth and Word Consciousness" by Rod Winters. Originally published in *The Reading Teacher*, Volume 6. Copyright © 2009 by International Reading Association. Reprinted by permission of John Wiley & Sons, Inc.
All rights reserved.

1 2 3 4 5 6 7 8 9 10   40   33 32 31 30 29 28 27 26 25 24

Scholastic Inc., 557 Broadway, New York, NY 10012

CONTENTS

ACKNOWLEDGMENTS

My deepest thanks go to Ray Coutu, who labored with me through this book, patiently offering sound, clear feedback and shepherding the project to completion, despite many challenges and roadblocks. I also thank Sarah Longhi and Tara Welty, along with the entire editorial and design team: Danny Miller, Tannaz Fassihi, Maria Lilja, and Samantha Unger.

Thanks to the schools that I have worked with and the children who have allowed me to work out many of these instructional ideas with them.

Also, gratitude to Mary Knight-McKenna for her feedback on Chapter 6 and to Michele Myers for feedback on Chapter 3.

Thank you to Ray Reutzel for the beautiful foreword, and to Doug Fisher, Kathleen Brown, Holly Lane, Matt Burns, Parvina Panghali, Laura Tortorelli, Pat Vadasy, and Sharon Walpole for their support.

I would also like to thank my Virginia Tech colleagues Dana Robertson, Donna Fortune, and Trevor Stewart for their patience and support.

Lastly, appreciation and gratitude go to my dear friend Rachel Klein, who across 25 years of friendship has taken my calls and listened to me, providing sound advice and guidance.

FOREWORD
by D. Ray Reutzel

D r. Heidi Anne Mesmer's *Big Words for Young Readers* is long overdue! After so much attention has been focused on teaching single-syllable words, it is high time to provide teachers with the help they need to deliver effective and motivating instruction in multisyllabic words and multimorphemic words. In other words, BIG WORDS!

I dare say, there has never been an elementary teacher who has not experienced that deer-in-the-headlights look students give when they encounter their first few big words. And now, thanks to Dr. Mesmer, there is finally a book to help them. It's a ready-to-use compendium of relevant, research-based, and practical guidance on teaching young readers to decode and understand big words. Dr. Mesmer writes in an accessible style—this is not a book that will sit on your shelf unused.

The first chapter, "Language Essentials—or What You Need to Know Without Becoming a Linguist!," is spot-on for today's focus on the science of reading and instruction inspired by it. Unfortunately, many elementary teachers are tempted to teach children everything they've learned from professional development trainings, as the science of reading has taken hold. Although many of those trainings are useful, the amount and type of information presented in them is far more than youngsters need to learn to read proficiently. Fortunately, Dr. Mesmer cuts to the nitty-gritty in her first chapter.

Chapter 2 provides a logically constructed, broad scope and sequence of skills for teaching big words. The scope and sequence suggests teaching compound words, contractions, and inflected endings in kindergarten and first grade, and teaching syllables and syllable types in first and second grades. Prefixes and suffixes are cued up for teaching in second through fourth grades, and Latin and Greek roots finish the job in fourth and fifth grades.

In Chapter 3, Dr. Mesmer does a nice job of presenting several commonly available and useful assessment tools for examining students' understanding of phonics and morphology: The Informal Decoding Inventory and the LETRS Phonics and Word Reading Survey, along with the widely accepted Upper-Level Spelling Inventory from *Words Their Way*. She then explains the Developmental Spelling Assessment and the MONSTER, P.I. to complete her recommendations for morphological assessments. She wraps up the chapter by discussing implications for multilingual learners and those with dialectical differences.

Chapter 4 serves up four perfectly blended, essential ingredients for big-word learning: 1) a big-words mindset, 2) curiosity, 3) skills, and 4) efficient and effective instruction. It then describes seven elements of efficient and effective instruction drawn directly from the available evidence in the science of reading (SOR) and learning sciences (LS) research bases.

Chapters 5–8 focus on the four major elements of the broad scope and sequence presented in Chapter 2. Dr. Mesmer begins each chapter with what to teach and then discusses when and how to teach it. I've seen few books that provide so many accessible, motivating, evidence-based teaching strategies and activities in so few pages. These chapters are treasure troves for teaching big words to young readers.

Lastly, don't just cruise by the appendix. There are multiple listings of big words, organized in myriad ways, that you will find very useful.

Once I opened this book, I could not put it down. Its design is clean, attractive, and easy to navigate. I plan to recommend it in all my professional development work across the nation to support the teaching of big words in elementary classrooms. It is a one-of-kind, go-to resource for teachers, professional developers, and teacher educators.

Congratulations to Scholastic and Dr. Mesmer on a wonderful contribution to the professional literature in early literacy. You deserve high praise for bringing considerable expertise to this topic and making it available to those of us who have long awaited such a resource.

—D. RAY REUTZEL
Distinguished Senior Research Fellow, Utah State University
Dean and Professor Emeritus, University of Wyoming
Member and Past President of the Reading Hall of Fame

Introduction

About four years ago, after finishing a book for K–2 teachers on phonics instruction, *Letter Lessons and First Words*, I began to have thoughts about writing this book. They began as nudges, insights about how K–2 phonics instruction could be improved. Then they expanded as I observed and worked with grade 3–5 students and watched what reading more complex texts required of them. Big words were a big part of what they had to do. Every third or fourth word in the texts they chose or were given seemed to have a prefix, suffix, or Latin root (e.g., *audience*, *presupposing*, *excitement*, *evaporation*), and knowing how to blend a simple CVC word was not helping them. As I talked with teachers about my observations, I realized that I was on to something: The field needed a pragmatic, research-based book on decoding and understanding big words, the whoppers that stumped kids while reading and caused them to freeze in their tracks.

Why I Wrote This Book for K–5 Teachers

Experiences like those lead to my four main reasons for writing this book.

Reason 1: To disrupt the pervasive tradition of K–2 instruction focusing on single-syllable, single-morpheme words

The first reason, as I mentioned, came about after I finished a K–2 phonics book. I was in a kindergarten room, probably in January, doing what most kindergarten teachers do at that time of year—modeling word decoding and allowing students to practice decoding in small groups. When the students in my little group got to the word *hats*, they started to struggle.

"Hat," said Zara, a perky, decisive little girl.

"Oh, that's not all of it. Look closely at the end," I said.

"It's got an *s*," Zara pointed out.

"Yes, so put it on the end of *hat*. How does that sound?"

"hat sss."

"Well, can you put it together?" (Zara continued to pronounce the base *hat* and the *s* with a pause between them.)

"Let's practice blending those together."

I modeled how to blend the sound at the end of *hats*—*ts*—until Zara got it and the lightbulb went off. "Hats!" she beamed, and we moved on. Later that day, I realized that I had missed an important opportunity to show Zara the purpose of that *s* and the meaning that it added to the word. The *s* is an inflection that shows that there was more than one hat. The *s* is a morpheme, and I could have taught her that, but I didn't.

So my first reason for writing this book was to disrupt the pervasive tradition of K–2 instruction focusing exclusively on words with only one syllable and one morpheme. As I detail in Chapter 5, this is simply not wise. Even in the early grades, students must decode and understand words that have multiple syllables and multiple morphemes.

Reason 2: To challenge the notion that single-syllable patterns are taught in K–2 and multiple-syllable patterns are taught in 3–5

My second reason for writing this book was to counter the notion that primary grades only involve single-syllable patterns and the intermediate grades only involve big words. I was seeing only professional books, including my own, focused on K–2 decoding and books focused on 3–5 structural analysis. I also saw K–5 teachers often working with *different* scope-and-sequence documents, which was fracturing communication and preventing vertical alignment. Teachers needed a resource that sketched out the parameters of big-words instruction, from kindergarten (yes, kindergarten!) to grade 5. Students' knowledge accumulates with effective instruction across days, weeks, months, and years. For that reason, I provide a broad K–5 scope and sequence, which I introduce in Chapter 2 and revisit in Chapters 4–8.

Reason 3: To make *morphology* part of our professional language, just like *phonics* and "phonological awareness"

My third reason for writing this book was inspired by the silence and blank stares I was receiving from teachers during professional development presentations. Whenever I started to talk about *morphemes*, the smallest meaningful units in a word (e.g., *brak-ing*, *act-ion*), that's the response I got: silence and blank stares. Teachers generally understood the meat of whatever I was talking about, but as soon as I uttered that word *morpheme*, I could feel the tension in the room. I realized that there was a missing piece in K–5 word instruction, *morphology*—and teachers were not comfortable with it, yet needed to be. *Morphology* should be part of our professional language, just like *phonics* and "phonological awareness."

Reason 4: To help you set the stage for morphological instruction in middle school, high school, and college

My fourth reason for writing this book was to help K–5 teachers prepare students for word-level instruction after elementary school. Morphological instruction should keep going. Elementary teachers have the important job of laying a foundation for more advanced instruction in later grades and beyond.

Understanding Content and Concepts

To decode and understand big words, students and teachers must understand basic linguistic content, such as how to add an inflection to a word (e.g., *batting*, *hiking*, *toasting*) and how to use Latin and Greek roots to expand words (e.g., *scrib/script-: scripture, prescribe, transcribe, transcript, describe*). Effective instruction involves explaining that content in understandable ways and showing students how to unpack words and use the morphemes to understand the meaning of words (e.g., *autobiography* = self, automatic + life + write). This book will help you do that.

When we teach big words, we are not only teaching students specific content, such as the meaning of a prefix (e.g., *pre* = before), but also the fact that some morphemes, such as prefixes, go at the beginning of words and change meaning. All morphemes do not do the same things. Some change a word's part of speech (e.g., the noun *terror* becomes the verb *terrorize* when *-ize* is added) and others don't (e.g., the nouns *hat* and *hats*, the adjectives *happy* and *happiest*). It's critical for you and your students to understand

How This Book Is Organized

Having been a classroom teacher for many years, I know firsthand how busy a teacher's life is. Who has time for reading dense, heavy professional books? I certainly didn't! I'd skim a chapter during lunch, flip to find an activity after dinner, and jot down its steps on sticky notes the next morning. So I took that to heart as I was writing. The book is organized into two parts.

Part I: Foundations of Teaching Big Words

Part I sets you up with the information you need:

- Language essentials for teaching big words (Chapter 1)
- A scope and sequence for teaching big words (Chapter 2)
- Tools for assessing students' knowledge of big words (Chapter 3)

Research tells us that teachers simply do not have the same understanding of the morphological elements of English as they do of the phonemic and graphemic elements (Cunningham et al., 2023; Tortorelli et al., 2021). That is why I wrote Chapter 1 in a succinct and, hopefully, clear style. The scope and sequence is based on a common K–5 sequence of word parts and found in many standards documents. It sketches a broad outline for instruction and is aligned to the activities in Part II. Assessment is critical to knowing where to start on the scope and sequence, so Chapter 3 describes several useful, formative assessments.

Part II: What to Teach, When to Teach It, and How to Teach It

Part II contains a chapter on general, research-based principles of teaching big words (Chapter 4), followed by four chapters that align with the scope and sequence to move you systematically through instruction:

- Compounds, contractions, and inflections without spelling changes in grades K–1 (Chapter 5)
- Syllables and syllable types in grades 1–2 (Chapter 6)
- Prefixes and suffixes in grades 2–4 (Chapter 7)
- Latin and Greek word roots in grades 4–5 (Chapter 8)

Each chapter contains a section called "What to Teach" that reviews the details of the particular word part. The second section in each chapter, "When to Teach It," connects the content to the broad scope and sequence. The last section of each chapter, "How to Teach It," contains research-informed teaching activities.

that English is not *just* about phonemes and graphemes. A morpheme is the smallest unit of meaning in a word—a whole word or a word part. When you encounter a big word, ideally, you look for morphemes, meaningful parts (e.g., *re-settle-ment*). Other concepts might include understanding that inflections don't change a word's part of speech (e.g., *girl/girls*; *grow/growing*; *big/bigger/biggest*), that compounds are two freestanding words combined (e.g., *headrest*), or that derivational suffixes provide us with ways to expand a word into different parts of speech (e.g., *excite*, *exciting*, *excitedly*, *excitement*).

Translating Research Findings Into Useful Information

In education, research is our North Star—our way of knowing what will work and what won't. Although carrying out research is a messy and ongoing process, it is important and useful. This book is grounded in solid reading research. I have read many studies and done my best to translate the findings of those studies into useful information for the classroom. The citations you see throughout the book and the reference list at the end of the book indicate that the content is reliable.

I hope you find *Big Words for Young Readers* accessible and engaging. May it encourage you to dive into big words, no matter what elementary grade you teach. I have found that with a basic understanding of language essentials, a scope and sequence, assessments, and activities, teachers' stress level diminishes, and they find themselves enjoying exploring big words, along with their students.

FOUNDATIONS OF TEACHING BIG WORDS

PART I

CHAPTER 1

Language Essentials— or What You Need to Know Without Becoming a Linguist!

When I was teaching fourth grade, I had a student named Javon, who was a strong reader. One day, while practicing a reader's theater script on Martin Luther King Jr., Javon was sailing along, adding all kinds of expression and phrasing to his reading until he came to the word *incredibly*. "In... in...," he tried and then looked to me for help. "Well, find a chunk," I directed. Seeing that didn't work, I went on to say, "Find the base word." A blank stare again. "See, the base word is *incredible*, and you add -*ly*. It's *incredibly*." At the time, I thought that was great, but it revealed a big problem that I had and that many teachers have.

My on-the-fly word prompting was not effective because I was not teaching morphology. Although it was not wrong to say that the word *incredible* was a base word, it reflected my lack of knowledge. The word *incredible* has a Latin root, *cred* (meaning believe) that combines with the prefix *in* (meaning not) to form the word *incredible* (not believable), with three parts. Had I been teaching Latin roots, I would have had him find *cred-*, which appears in many words (e.g., *credit*, *discredit*, *credibility*), and then locate the prefixes and suffixes added to it. My scattershot instruction was "giving Javon a fish," and not "teaching him how to fish."

It all starts with understanding how the English language works. You cannot teach something that you do not know exists or that you do not understand. Knowing linguistic content is not enough to teach big words, but it's a good place to start. That's why Chapters 5–8 begin with "What to Teach" sections that explain the word parts and how they work. Just as you need to know terms such as *digraph, short vowel,* and *phonemic awareness* to teach reading, you need to know terms such as *derivational suffix, inflection, morpheme,* and *syllable type,* too. That's where this book comes in!

We need succinct labels for complex concepts for three reasons:

1. Labels are important for professional growth. They expand our mental maps of word structures, clarifying differences that are meaningful for teaching.

2. They can be useful in explaining concepts to kids (e.g., *prefix, base word*).

3. They allow us to convey concepts without explanations that are too laborious and inefficient.

For example, instead of saying, "I am going to teach about when a vowel says its own name," we use the label *long vowel.* There is a vocabulary for teaching big words as well.

Beyond Phonemes and Graphemes: Letters Build Larger Sound and Meaning Units

When I talk to teachers about foundational skills, they use words such as *phoneme* and *grapheme* effortlessly. They know that English writing is alphabetic, a system of coding speech sounds, or *phonemes*, by using *graphemes* or visual letter symbols.

Imagine asking a student to sound out letter by letter an eight-phoneme word such as *masterful*. That is not the way to approach that word. Instead, the skilled reader looks for parts, base words, prefixes, suffixes, and syllables. So why not teach kids to do that?

In English, there are more long words than short words (Balota et al., 2007), and children cannot get past primary-grade texts if they understand only the phoneme/grapheme, letter-by-letter alphabetic layer. Graphemes build larger units, and skilled readers consolidate grapheme-based units as they decode (Ehri, 2005).

Big words in English have two different and sometimes overlapping parts: syllables (e.g., *un-but-ton*, *an-i-mals*) and morphemes (e.g., *un-button*, *animal-s*). Let's start with the part that may be more familiar to you.

Sound Units: Syllables

Syllables are units of sound, units of pronunciation, that are made up of one or more phonemes. They have a vowel sound, called the "nucleus," even if that sound is sometimes represented by a consonant (e.g., *fry*). A syllable can be formed with just one vowel by itself, or with one or more consonants at the beginning or end (e.g., *a-bout*, *see*, *or-gan-ize*, *stripe*, *test*, *stretch*). Most syllables have a vowel letter (Eide, 2012). The vowel sounds in syllables are made with an open mouth and the sound can be sustained (e.g., /a/ vs. /b/). Sometimes the sounds /l/ or /r/ will form a syllable in English (e.g., *battle*, *acre*).

In the following example, the word *organ* has two syllables, one with a vowel sound at the beginning (*or*) and one with a vowel sound closed off by consonants (*gan*). Six syllable types based on the vowel are often used.

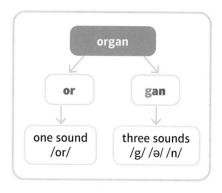

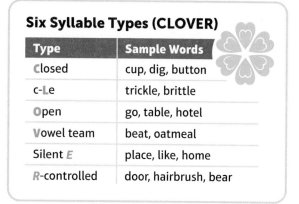

Six Syllable Types (CLOVER)

Type	Sample Words
Closed	cup, dig, button
c-**L**e	trickle, brittle
Open	go, table, hotel
Vowel team	beat, oatmeal
Silent **E**	place, like, home
R-controlled	door, hairbrush, bear

Some syllable types can also be *simple* or *complex*. A simple syllable has single consonants, and a complex syllable has consonant blends at the beginning or end (e.g., *str-*, *-nt*, *gl-*). If you add in a few consonants at the beginning or end of *bag*, then it becomes a complex syllable—like *bang* or or *brag*. (See Chapter 6 for more information on syllable types.)

Meaning Units: Morphemes

A morpheme is a unit of meaning that may or may not stand alone. All words have at least one morpheme. Morphemes add some level of meaning (e.g., *-ly*, *cred*, *-ed*, *-s*, *-ment*). The morpheme is the smallest unit of sound that carries meaning in a word. This is not to be confused with *phonemes,* which are the smallest sound units in words.

A morpheme can be an entire word (e.g., *cat*) or just a part (e.g., *-s*) So, in the word *cats* there are two morphemes: 1) *cat*, which tells us it's an animal, and 2) *-s*, which tells us there's more than one of them.

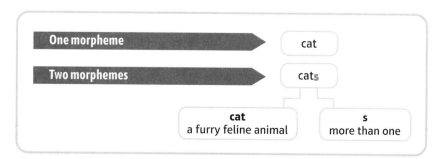

A morpheme is a unit of meaning that cannot be divided into smaller units of meaning (Jump & Johnson, 2022). You cannot break *cat* into smaller *meaning* parts. It is not as if the *ca* tells us that it's a four-legged animal and the *t* tells us it's an animal with fur. The word *cat* is the smallest meaningful part.

Morphemes are the building blocks of meaning (Henry, 2019). That means readers use them to decode words and understand their meanings. When readers unpack *rerunning*, for example, they use the prefix *re* to decode the word and to understand that the action is happening again. The open syllable *re* is not just a syllable, but also a morpheme because it carries meaning. However, remember that the letters *re* are not a morpheme in every word.

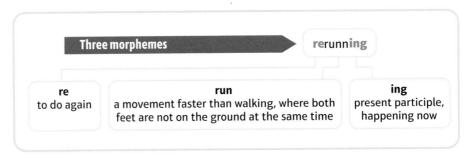

Three morphemes		rerunning
re to do again	**run** a movement faster than walking, where both feet are not on the ground at the same time	**ing** present participle, happening now

When teaching a morpheme, identify it and ask students to find its meaning. Sometimes they will see adjacent letters in a word that match those in the morpheme (e.g., *re*). However, that does not necessarily mean those letters serve as a morpheme. The key is to ask if the word part adds meaning.

Why is that important? As we clarify word parts, we learn what something *is* by learning what it is *not*. So you learn what the morpheme *re* is by learning what it is not. Sometimes *re* is part of a syllable in a single-morpheme word (e.g., *rep*tile) or part of a vowel team (e.g., *rea*der). That's why we cannot

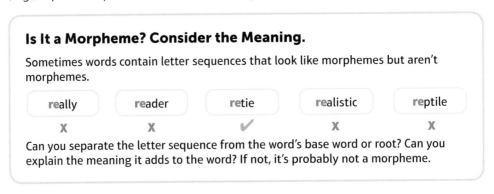

Is It a Morpheme? Consider the Meaning.

Sometimes words contain letter sequences that look like morphemes but aren't morphemes.

really	reader	retie	realistic	reptile
X	X	✔	X	X

Can you separate the letter sequence from the word's base word or root? Can you explain the meaning it adds to the word? If not, it's probably not a morpheme.

simply tell students to look for letter sequences when teaching morphology. They must think about meaning and if the letter sequence is a morpheme that adds meaning or not. You cannot teach morphology without talking about meaning.

There are two categories of morphemes: free morphemes and bound morphemes.

Free Morphemes

Free morphemes are also stand-alone words. They fall into two groups, content words—nouns, verbs, adjectives, and adverbs—or function words—conjunctions, prepositions, pronouns, articles, and auxiliary verbs. When we are reading, content words convey most of the text's meaning.

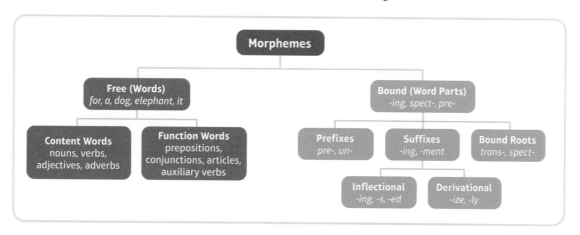

Bound Morphemes

Bound morphemes are meaningful units that cannot stand alone and, therefore, must be attached to other morphemes. There are three types of bound morphemes: bound roots, which are from Latin and Greek, prefixes, and suffixes. The term *affixes* is an umbrella term for prefixes and suffixes. A bound root is the part of a multimorphemic word that carries the main meaning, but usually does not form a recognizable English word (e.g., *cred-*: *incredible, credit*). There are two types of suffixes: inflectional and derivational. Inflectional suffixes are added to words to show verb tense (e.g., *fix-ing*) or number (e.g., *cat-s*), or to compare (e.g., *green-er, green-est*). Derivational suffixes are added to words to change their part of speech (e.g., *act*: verb, *act-ion*: noun. (See Chapters 7 and 8 for more on affixes and bound roots.)

Morphology Bridges Word Recognition and Language Comprehension

If you follow trends in literacy instruction, you know that the Simple View of Reading (Hoover & Gough, 1990) and the Reading Rope (Scarborough, 2001) are used to explain skilled reading. These models are handy ways for us to think about the parts of reading. But what do they say about multisyllabic and multimorphemic words?

The Simple View of Reading

The Simple View of Reading, a research-tested model, contains two parts: 1) independently recognizing/decoding words, and 2) comprehending the individual and collective meanings of those words (Hoover & Gough, 1990).

When students read, they independently decode words. They look at the print and pronounce the words orally or in their heads without help. If students cannot decode a book's words on their own, if you have to decode the words for them, they are not reading. Reading requires independent recognition of words. Perhaps using morphology and knowledge of syllables is covered in the word recognition part of the Simple View, but neither is mentioned in the theory.

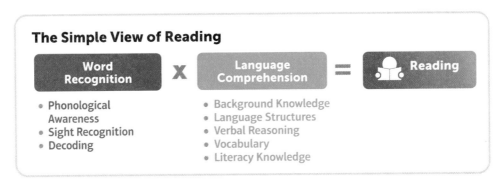

The Simple View of Reading

Word Recognition **X** Language Comprehension **=** Reading

- Phonological Awareness
- Sight Recognition
- Decoding

- Background Knowledge
- Language Structures
- Verbal Reasoning
- Vocabulary
- Literacy Knowledge

The second part of the Simple View focuses on language comprehension. In testing the model, researchers considered comprehension separately from decoding. So, they tested listening comprehension. They read passages to readers to determine what they *might* be able to understand if they could decode all the words. This theory has been tested and retested over the years (Gough & Tunmer, 1986; Hoover & Tunmer, 2018, 2020; Nation, 2019). Many researchers have also contested it or amended it. Teachers should have some understanding of this model because it is the basis of the Reading Rope (Scarborough, 2001) and the Active View of Reading (Duke & Cartwright, 2021).

The Reading Rope

To break down the processes of skilled reading even further, Scarborough developed the Reading Rope. Word recognition relies on phonological awareness, decoding, and sight recognition (or automatically knowing a word without decoding it). Language comprehension, developed first at the spoken level, revolves around a child's background knowledge, verbal reasoning, vocabulary, understanding of language structures (syntax), and literacy knowledge (e.g., different genres of text, print concepts). Yet, this model and the Simple View do not explicitly address morphology.

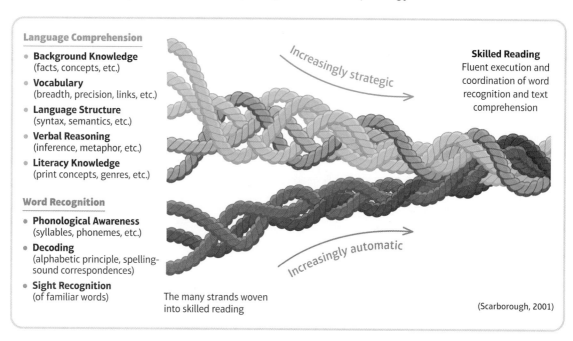

Language Comprehension

- **Background Knowledge** (facts, concepts, etc.)
- **Vocabulary** (breadth, precision, links, etc.)
- **Language Structure** (syntax, semantics, etc.)
- **Verbal Reasoning** (inference, metaphor, etc.)
- **Literacy Knowledge** (print concepts, genres, etc.)

Word Recognition

- **Phonological Awareness** (syllables, phonemes, etc.)
- **Decoding** (alphabetic principle, spelling-sound correspondences)
- **Sight Recognition** (of familiar words)

Increasingly strategic

Skilled Reading
Fluent execution and coordination of word recognition and text comprehension

Increasingly automatic

The many strands woven into skilled reading

(Scarborough, 2001)

The Active View of Reading

The Active View of Reading, which builds upon the Simple View and the Reading Rope, does address morphology among other aspects of reading (Duke & Cartwright, 2021). Morphology, the understanding of meaningful parts of words, is a "bridging process" connecting word recognition and language comprehension. This is a perfect way to understand morphology!

Morphology has one "foot" in word recognition because seeing and pronouncing meaningful word parts *is* word recognition. And morphology has one foot in language comprehension. To understand the word *capitalize*, the skilled reader accesses the meanings of those morphemes. *Capital* means wealth or money and *-ize* is the act of. Thus, the meaning of the word *capitalize* is the act of creating or making money or wealth.

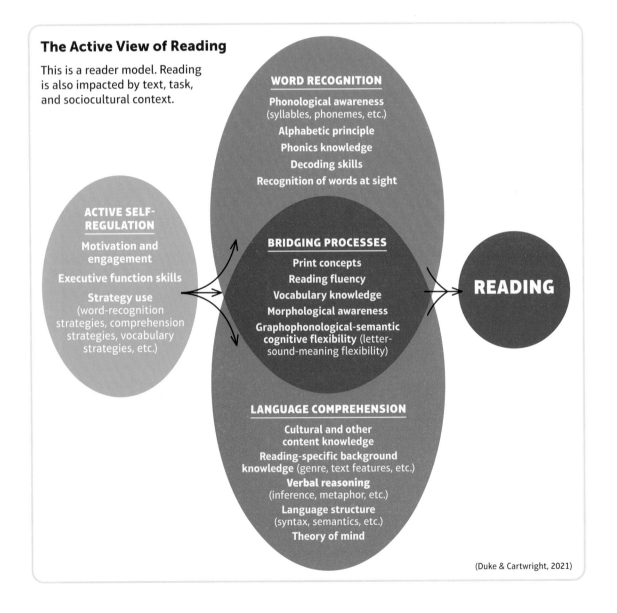

The Active View of Reading

This is a reader model. Reading is also impacted by text, task, and sociocultural context.

WORD RECOGNITION
Phonological awareness (syllables, phonemes, etc.)
Alphabetic principle
Phonics knowledge
Decoding skills
Recognition of words at sight

ACTIVE SELF-REGULATION
Motivation and engagement
Executive function skills
Strategy use (word-recognition strategies, comprehension strategies, vocabulary strategies, etc.)

BRIDGING PROCESSES
Print concepts
Reading fluency
Vocabulary knowledge
Morphological awareness
Graphophonological-semantic cognitive flexibility (letter-sound-meaning flexibility)

READING

LANGUAGE COMPREHENSION
Cultural and other content knowledge
Reading-specific background knowledge (genre, text features, etc.)
Verbal reasoning (inference, metaphor, etc.)
Language structure (syntax, semantics, etc.)
Theory of mind

(Duke & Cartwright, 2021)

Meaning and word recognition are inseparable when readers access morphology. Readers are using both at the same time. They use meaningful word parts to decode a word and they use those parts to understand a word. So, morphology is both. As researchers Duke and Cartwright (2021) explain, "Importantly, morphological awareness provides a clear counter to the notion that we can develop reading simply by working on word recognition and oral language, as morphological awareness has a particular value in written text."

Morphology instruction is indeed a "missing" link and yet research has shown that instruction in morphology impacts vocabulary and spelling (Bowers et al., 2010; Goodwin & Ahn, 2013). In fact, systematic morphological instruction should be started earlier rather than later.

Historical Influences on English

As hard as it may be to believe, English did not originate in England but from Germanic tribes, the Anglo-Saxons who invaded what is now known as the British Isles, starting around the year 450 (Henry, 2010). The Germanic words they brought were used to label simple, everyday things (e.g., *field*, *milk*) and actions, and formed the base or foundation of English.

In 1066, the Normans, or French, invaded the British Isles and brought with them Latin words that they themselves had gotten from the Romans, effectively laying the second layer of English. The Latin words were more sophisticated, introducing ideas and concepts that were more formal and were used in education (e.g., *confident*, *preventative*). Languages influenced by Roman Latin are called Romance languages (e.g., French, Spanish, English).

Later, the Romans borrowed words from the Greeks, adding the last layer of English. Greek roots were even more sophisticated, encapsulating concepts in science and math (e.g., *thermometer*, *centimeter*). Typically, primary students initially learn words with an Anglo-Saxon base when acquiring the basic phoneme-grapheme relationships and later begin to acquire the more sophisticated Latin and Greek elements.

Anglo-Saxon (Germanic Tribes)
- One-syllable, everyday words (e.g., *bed*, *sit*)

Norman (French via Romans)
- Latin words borrowed from Romans
- Formal words of education (e.g., *extracted*, *defendant*)

Greek (via Romans)
- Technical words of math and science
- Combining forms (e.g., *telephoto*, *biology*)

In Closing, Remember...

Morphology has not received enough attention in K–5 literacy instruction, and yet, even in the early grades, students learn how to attack big words. Here are a few points to keep in mind.

- English is not just about phoneme-grapheme relationships, but morphology as well. In elementary school, we hit the nail on the head with phonics. But understanding phonics is not enough to be a successful reader. English is morpho-phonemic, meaning that the sound-spellings that we teach students form meaning units that are important to understand in longer words. When students read a word, such as *repopulate*, they should look for meaningful parts.

- Early literacy instruction focuses on teaching the phoneme-grapheme relationships in English, but it should also focus on the second layer of English writing—the morpheme.

- Educators use syllable types to help students decode multisyllabic words. As students advance, they are best served by finding the morphemes in words.

Which Ones and When? A Scope and Sequence for Teaching Big Words

L i Lin, a teacher in Sacramento, California, recently moved from first grade to fourth grade and expected more direction on how to help students decode and understand big words. She explains:

I knew there would be a greater focus on vocabulary and comprehension in fourth grade, and honestly, I was happy to move away from sounding out words and so much phonemic awareness. I wanted to dive into comprehending books about oceans or reading chapter books with my students.

But I was unprepared for their difficulties in decoding long words. The worst part was there wasn't much guidance in the standards or teachers' editions. In first grade, teaching standards are so specific. In fact, it's almost overkill. But in fourth grade, the materials are so vague. Directions say things like, "Teach common prefixes, suffixes, and word roots." Okay, so which ones and when? I did not have much to go on, and I felt overwhelmed.

Li Lin's experience is familiar. Because of decades of intense focus on phonics, scope-and-sequence documents for early decoding are much more helpful, complete, and precise (sometimes too much!). Similarly, the K–2 standards for foundational skills in Li Lin's state contain a great deal of linguistic content (e.g., blends, silent *e*, consonant digraphs), but the fourth- and fifth-grade standards contain just one sentence about decoding: "Use combined knowledge of all letter-sound correspondences, syllabication patterns, and morphology (e.g., roots and affixes) to read accurately unfamiliar multisyllabic words in context and out of context." Everything is thrown into that standard but the kitchen sink! Upper-elementary teachers have had to figure out what to do on their own.

Systematic, Explicit Instruction Requires a Scope and Sequence

Reading science has clearly established that *systematic*, *explicit* instruction is most effective for teaching word-level skills (Bowers et al., 2010; Goodwin & Ahn, 2013). Systematic instruction means following a scope and sequence—a road map of sorts, telling you the routes to take and turns to make to help students decode and understand words.

Systematic

Following a scope and sequence, a "road map," which tells you:

- Content to be taught (e.g., common prefixes, common Latin roots)
- Order of content, from easier to harder

Explicit

Directly telling students relationships between spellings and sounds and meaning:

"The prefix *in-* usually means *not*, like in the word *incorrect*. Sometimes it can mean *within*, like in the word *insight*."

Explicit instruction means using direct, clear language to tell students how the spellings of words relate to sounds and, more importantly, meanings. As explained in Chapter 1, the morphological principle in English means that spellings maintain meaning, or morphological relationships, across words, even when pronunciations change. That's why we spell words such as *sign*, *signal*, and *signature* similarly, even though they do not all sound the same.

Everyone seems to have gotten the message that K–2 phonics instruction should be systematic and explicit, but often K–2 instruction focuses only on single-syllable words, not big words. And, in grades 3–5, Li Lin's experience is typical: Systematic, explicit instruction in big words dwindles. In fact, often big-words instruction is anything but explicit and systematic. It's *implicit* and *embedded*. When instruction is implicit, the teacher is using indirect and, likely, unclear language. Students have to kind of figure things out on their own. When instruction is embedded, the teacher is not following a scope and sequence, and instead is teaching parts randomly, as they come up while reading. For example, if the word *inflexible* comes up, the teacher gives instruction on the prefix *in-*, and then the next day, if the word *creation* comes up, the teacher moves to *-ion*. The instruction is driven by what comes up by chance and does not follow a scope and sequence that organizes parts by difficulty or similarity. Lastly, I have noticed that few scope and sequence documents for big words cover all the elementary grades, and yet, a seamless K–5 scope and sequence vertically aligns instruction across grades and enhances communication.

In Chapter 1, I covered basic information about morphemes and syllables. In this chapter, I take that information a step further by providing a scope and sequence. After all, without one, instruction cannot be effective.

A K–5 Scope and Sequence for Big Words

There are detailed scope-and-sequence documents at different grades that can guide big-words instruction, with content organized into categories (e.g., inflections, roots, suffixes) and lists of words to guide weekly instruction (Moats & Tolman, 2019; Ganske, 2020; Bear et al., 2020). The National Curriculum in English in the United Kingdom goes so far as to offer statutory content and includes word lists. That is not what I am providing here.

A Broad Scope and Sequence

The scope and sequence on the next page is a broad listing of word parts, including both morphemes and syllable types, found in standards documents from several states as well as the Common Core State Standards for the English Language Arts. It shows a loose sequence by word part (e.g., compound words, inflections, contractions, syllable types, prefixes, and suffixes) that most teachers are required to teach. You can see how parts progress from simple to complex. Chapter 5 covers compound words, contractions, and inflections without spelling changes. The first big words that students encounter are compound words based on their knowledge

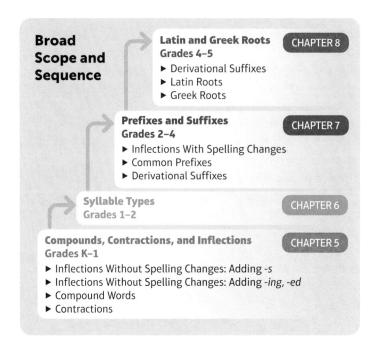

Broad Scope and Sequence

Latin and Greek Roots
Grades 4–5 CHAPTER 8
- ▸ Derivational Suffixes
- ▸ Latin Roots
- ▸ Greek Roots

Prefixes and Suffixes
Grades 2–4 CHAPTER 7
- ▸ Inflections With Spelling Changes
- ▸ Common Prefixes
- ▸ Derivational Suffixes

Syllable Types
Grades 1–2 CHAPTER 6

Compounds, Contractions, and Inflections
Grades K–1 CHAPTER 5
- ▸ Inflections Without Spelling Changes: Adding *-s*
- ▸ Inflections Without Spelling Changes: Adding *-ing, -ed*
- ▸ Compound Words
- ▸ Contractions

of decoding (e.g., *sunset, uphill, catnap*). Early on, students can also learn inflections that require no spelling changes, such as adding an *-s* to *pig* or an *-ing* to a word such as *fish*. Students also learn contractions. Once students have mastered decoding vowels in single-syllable words, they learn syllable types so that they can decode multisyllabic words. (See Chapter 6.) Chapter 7 pivots to prefixes and suffixes and circles back to inflectional suffixes that require spelling changes (e.g., *nodding, roping, cried*). Also in Chapter 7 are common prefixes and derivational suffixes (e.g., *-ion, -ily*). Finally, students begin to learn Latin and Greek roots, which continues into high school and beyond. (See Chapter 8.)

A scope and sequence is simply a continuum. You use assessments to locate where students are on it so that you can offer the instruction they need. (See Chapter 3 for more on assessment.) The scope and sequence I offer is a loose plan based on standards that are widely used in the United States. The grades suggested follow overall patterns that you will see but individual states and programs differ. Use the guidance that your district and state require you to use.

Essential Points

In shaping the broad scope and sequence, I kept in mind a few essential points.

Recognize that basic phonics is the foundation of big words.

Whether students can read morphologically complex words, such as *disorganized*, depends on their abilities to read base words (e.g. *organize*) and the vowel patterns in those base words (e.g., *or-gan-ize*) (Goodwin et al., 2013; Goodwin et al., 2014). In other words, if students do not know that *-igh* represents the long *i* sound (as in *sight*), they will not be able to read an *-igh* word with inflections and/or affixes (as in *insightful*). Students must know the many vowel patterns in English spelling (e.g., *ee, ea, ey, e_e*) to read big words.

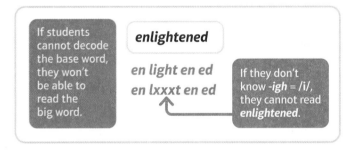

In one study, researchers asked struggling fourth and fifth graders to review vowel patterns (e.g., *ea, oo, oa, oi*) *before* working on affixes (Toste et al., 2019).

Do All Students Within a Grade Need the Same Big-Words Content?

Not every student in a given grade needs grade-level material. Although reading development is highly predictable, children move through stages at different rates (Kuhn & Stahl, 2022). For example, one third-grade teacher might find a group of students that needs more support with inflections and is not ready for derivational suffixes. Morphological content should be taught based on the assessments described in Chapter 3. Blindly following a grade-based scope and sequence is not an effective way to teach students, especially students who might not be at the same place as their classmates or who may have gaps in their knowledge or need review. Multilingual learners may need additional support and modeling. That's why elementary teachers need *one* scope and sequence, so that they can back up or move forward based on what students need. Some first graders are reading texts with derivational suffixes and need that, and some third graders are still working on inflections.

Apply the research on patterns that appear in texts students read.

In designing a scope and sequence, developers can lean on research that identifies the morphemes and syllable patterns that appear in books commonly read by children in grades 1–5.

Grade 1: In first grade, over 40 percent of words have more than one syllable (Kearns & Hiebert, 2022), suggesting that teaching multisyllabic words is a must, starting as early as first grade. What do first-grade big words look like? They are usually common and contain only one morpheme (e.g., *different*, *children*, *elephant*). About 13 percent of those words contained multiple morphemes—mostly words with inflections (e.g., *-ing*, *-ed*, *-s*, *-ies*, *-er*), simple prefixes (e.g., *precook*, *return*), or compound words (e.g., *bathtub*, *girlfriend*) (Kearns & Hiebert, 2022).

Grades 3–5: In third grade and above, 60–80 percent of words in books children read are morphologically complex (e.g., *odorous*, *impreciseness*, *revolution*) (Nagy & Anderson, 1984). As texts get more advanced, less common words and affixes appear (e.g., *superlative*, *descendance*). That is why morphological instruction continues through high school.

Organize instruction by morpheme type.

Different morphemes do different things. It's not just the word part's meaning you are teaching, but also its function. Our brains like to file information categorically. Teach groups of morphemes of the same type across a specific time, instead of skipping around. For example, you might teach common prefixes for three weeks (e.g., *un-*, *re-*, *in-/il-/im-*), helping students to understand the semantic information they add to the beginning of words. Then you might pivot to derivational suffixes for four weeks (e.g., *-er/-or*, *-ion/-tion*, *-ible/able*), helping students to understand how suffixes can change a base word's part of speech. Then you might move to a six-week unit on Latin and Greek roots (e.g., *vis-*, *cred-*, *bene-*, *spect-*). If you move from one type of morpheme to another too abruptly, students will struggle to understand the purposes of different morphemes.

So, approach them with caution!

Grade-by-Grade Content

I discuss the content by grade levels because it's important to understand what is commonly expected as students move through elementary school. If I am a first-grade teacher, I need to understand what content is typically covered. Notice that chapters are organized by *types* of word parts (e.g., Chapter 6, syllable types; Chapter 7, prefixes and suffixes). However, in most grades, teachers teach several types of word parts. For example, a first-grade teacher may teach compound words, inflections without spelling changes, contractions, and syllable types.

Big-words content should "spiral." In other words, a part will be introduced in one grade and then revisited and reinforced in the next. For example, derivational suffixes are introduced in grade 3 but, because they are quite complex, will be taught in grades 4 and 5 as well.

Kindergarten

Kindergartners are just learning how to read. They are learning their letter sounds and blending those sounds to decode simple words, as early as mid-year. Is big-words instruction appropriate for them? It is! Although most of their instruction will focus on single-syllable words made up of one morpheme, they can still learn some big-words concepts.

For example, as soon as they know how to decode a CVC pattern, students can learn decodable compounds made up of two CVC words (e.g., *suntan*, *bedbug*). They can also learn to read words with the inflectional -*s* ending, especially those that don't require spelling changes, which sometimes has the /z/ sound (e.g., *dogs*) and other times the /s/ sound (e.g., *cats*).

First Grade

Most first graders are still acquiring the basics of short vowels, along with consonant blends, digraphs, and vowel teams. They also benefit from learning decodable compounds that use those elements (e.g., *snowball*, *lunchbox*, *birdbath*). In first grade, we usually teach inflectional endings where there are no spelling changes (e.g., *lick: licking*, *licker*, and *licked*) (Bear et al., 2020; Henry, 2019). Lastly, first graders typically learn the six syllable types: open, closed, silent *e*, vowel teams, *r*-controlled, and consonant *-le*, which are acquired mainly as they learn vowel patterns, such as *or*, *ir*, *ar*, *ea*, *oa*, *o_e*, etc.

Second Grade

Second grade is a time to review and solidify syllable types. Syllable types should get a great deal of attention, and they can be applied to multisyllabic words where useful (e.g., *basket*, *garden*, *river*). In addition, students should learn how to add inflections to words when there are spelling changes (e.g., change *y* to *i*—*cries*, doubling—*hemmed*). The new content in second grade is common prefixes and suffixes, which are listed in Chapter 7. Prefixes will likely

be new to second graders because students are more familiar with suffixes. About half of the 20 most frequent prefixes listed in Chapter 7 are a good place to start.

Third Grade

Third grade is packed full of new expectations for readers. Students are building knowledge in the content areas, and they are reading extended texts. In third grade, review inflections with spelling changes to make sure that this content is solid. After being introduced to the most common prefixes in second grade, students will need more time to learn the less common ones. Several prefixes vary in meaning based on use (e.g., *in-* (not) vs. *in-* (within)). In third grade, derivational suffixes are introduced (e.g., *-ify*, *-ize*), and will continue into fourth grade because there are a lot of them.

Fourth and Fifth Grade

Students in grades 4 and 5 have similar needs because the content in these grades is similar and spirals from one to the next. As discussed in Chapters 7 and 8, derivational suffixes and Latin and Greek roots are introduced in the late elementary grades, and continue throughout high school because so many are related to disciplines (e.g., *hydro/a*, *therm*, *bio*, *crat/cracy*). In grades 4 and 5, students move into a kind of problem-solving approach by considering all morphological elements. For example, the Common Core State Standards for grades 4 and 5 ask students to "use combined knowledge of all letter-sound correspondences, syllabication patterns, and morphology (e.g., roots and affixes) to read accurately unfamiliar multisyllabic words in context and out of context."

In Closing, Remember...

Systematic instruction simply cannot happen without a solid scope and sequence. In this chapter, I presented a broad scope and sequence to guide instruction and provide more specific guidance in Chapters 5–8. Keep the following points in mind.

- Although my scope and sequence is organized sequentially by word parts, recognize that instruction should spiral. The chapters in this book focus on compounds, contractions, inflections, syllable types, prefixes and suffixes, and Latin and Greek roots, but these parts are introduced in one grade and then repeated, and developed in subsequent grades. Inflections without spelling changes get introduced in K–1, but are then revisited with spelling changes in second grade. This is a quality of strong instruction because knowledge accumulates and builds.
- Basic phonics, which focuses on phoneme-grapheme relationships, is the foundation of learning morphemes.
- Derivational suffixes and Latin and Greek roots should be introduced in elementary school and continue into high school.

CHAPTER 3

Assessments for Determining What Students Know— and Don't Know— About Big Words

A solid scope and sequence is a road map for instruction— the steps for you to follow to get students from where they are now to where they need to be. But a road map is no good if you don't know where you are in the first place! And that's one reason we have assessments—to determine a starting point for instruction based on what students know and don't know. With assessments, we don't waste time teaching content that students have already mastered, which is frustrating and tedious for students and teachers alike.

Assessments also help us to determine the effects of our efforts! Teaching does not always lead to learning. High-quality practice is a constant feedback loop of instruction, assessment, and reteaching as necessary. A solid assessment helps us determine how well our instruction is working. After all, there's no use worrying about explicit, systematic instruction if you have no idea what students have learned or need to learn.

Just as a reminder, the scope and sequence for big words in K–5 addresses compound words, inflections with and without spelling changes, contractions, syllable types, prefixes, derivational suffixes, and Latin and Greek roots. The assessments recommended in this chapter cover those word parts, but be forewarned: There are not as many K–5 assessments that focus on morphology. Most focus on spelling or decoding words with multiple syllables and morphemes, but not on students' insights about how morphemes work or contribute to meaning. In this section, I highlight three types of assessments:

- Decoding inventories
- Spelling inventories
- Morphological assessments

Decoding Inventories

Several decoding inventories ask students to decode multisyllabic words and words with multiple morphemes (Moats & Tolman, 2019; Walpole et al., 2019). Easy to administer, they consist of lists of real words and nonsense words that contain increasingly complex units. The teacher asks individual students to read the words while marking those the student decodes correctly and those he or she mispronounces. Usually, these inventories take about 10 minutes to administer and about five minutes to score.

The Informal Decoding Inventory

The Informal Decoding Inventory is an assessment that includes big words. Part I of the inventory covers letters and patterns in single-syllable words. Part II covers multisyllabic-word reading with 10 real words and 10 nonsense words in each of these categories: 1) compound words, 2) closed syllables, 3) open syllables, 4) vowel/consonant -e, 5) r-controlled syllables, 6) vowel teams, and 7) consonant -le.

The Informal Decoding Inventory is easy to administer and score, and the nonsense words provide a solid estimate of the degree to which a student might be able to decode unfamiliar real words. It covers syllable types well. For mastery level, the level indicating that no instruction is needed, students must correctly decode 80 percent of the real words and 60 percent of the nonsense words. This adjustment is because students typically perform slightly lower on nonsense words. The Informal Decoding Inventory does not measure advanced morphology and because it is given one-on-one, it takes a bit longer to administer. Also remember multisyllabic nonsense words can be challenging, and teachers need to review the pronunciations of each on their own before administering the assessment. The syllable types of assessment items in this measure are all words with multiple syllables and thus, estimate students' abilities to apply syllable types to decoding words. The assessment is useful for students who are applying syllable types to two- and three-syllable words, after they have learned all the types. (See Chapter 6.)

The LETRS Phonics and Word Reading Survey

The LETRS Phonics and Word Reading Survey contains sections on letters and high-frequency words, and over 100 words covering syllable types in one- and two-syllable words, inflected words, and those with derivational morphemes (Moats & Tolman, 2019). The teacher asks individual students to decode each word within three seconds.

The survey contains single-syllable words for each syllable type (except for open syllable) including two sections for closed syllables—one with simple syllables (e.g., *wed*, *napkin*) and one with complex syllables (e.g., *clamp*, *maddest*). For each syllable type there are three sets of words:

- real single-syllable words (e.g., *dome*, *fur*)
- pseudo single-syllable words (e.g., *pruse*, *glate*, *twun*, *blung*)
- multisyllabic words with the syllable type (e.g., *rabbit*, *upswing*, *cheater*)

The last section, which contains 28 words, covers inflections and common suffixes, compound words, and prefixes, roots, and derivational suffixes.

The LETRS Phonics and Word Reading Survey is easy to deliver

Decoding Inventories: Advantages and Disadvantages

- Measure a student's ability to decode words with different syllable types and/or multiple morphemes
- Contain lots of items related to syllable types; good for estimating knowledge of them
- LETRS Part II has 20+ items with inflections, derivational morphemes, and affixes.

- Take time because they're individually administered
- Do not test for understanding of the meanings of morphemes

and score. The syllable types elements work for students learning the syllable types in single-syllable words and in two-syllable words (Chapter 6). In addition, the inflections section would be useful for students learning to decode and spell inflections with spelling changes (Chapter 7). The five items with prefixes (Chapter 7), derivational suffixes (Chapter 7), and roots (Chapter 8) may give some insight into students' knowledge of these parts.

Overall, the decoding inventories do provide good information about students' abilities to decode words with multiple syllables and morphemes. The extensive lists of words with various syllable types make LETRS Phonics and Word Reading Survey especially suited to assess students who are working on syllable types. LETRS also has items for inflections and derivational suffixes.

Spelling Inventories

One straightforward way to assess students' knowledge of big words is to administer a spelling inventory (Bear et al., 2020; Ganske, 2020). The words in the assessment were selected specifically to test students' skills at various levels of complexity. Teachers dictate the words along with sentences, and students spell words.

The Upper-Level Spelling Inventory

The Upper-Level Spelling Inventory from *Words Their Way* (Bear et al., 2020) contains a collection of words that sample different word parts, moving from inflections to derivational suffixes to words with Latin and Greek roots. For example, the words *trapped*, *knotted*, *shaving*, and *scratches* test whether students know how to add the inflectional endings *-ed*, *-ing*, and *-es* to words. The words *fortunate*, *visible*, *circumference*, and *civilization* test knowledge of Latin and Greek roots. For each item, a part or parts of the word is/are listed based on the morphemic feature being tested. So, in the word *knotted,* the *kn* pattern, *-tted* (doubling inflection pattern), and short *o* are being tested. Students only need to spell the part of the word being tested to receive points. If they spelled the word *notted*, they would get the points for the inflection (*tted*), but not for the silent *k*. Points are assigned for each spelling and then totaled at the bottom of the morphemic feature column.

The Developmental Spelling Assessment

The Developmental Spelling Assessment (Ganske, 2020) contains a screening test and diagnostic test. The screening test helps the teacher get a ballpark estimate of which category or type of morpheme needs attention (e.g., inflections with spelling changes) and the diagnostic test pinpoints more precisely the patterns that a student knows (e.g., *hoping* = drop *e*, *tipping* = doubling, *fried* = change the *y* to *i*). The diagnostic test has more items per pattern. For example, there are five word items to test adding inflections, doubling, and *e*-drop with *ed* and *ing*. But scoring takes more time because you first give a screening measure and then a specific test based on the student's level. Also, like the other spelling inventories, you must score each word, sometimes for multiple elements.

There are several advantages of spelling inventories. First, they set a high bar for testing students' knowledge. Spelling is synthesis, meaning that students start without anything there (e.g., no printed word on the page) and must pull together their knowledge of words to create something—an accurate spelling. Second, spelling inventories are easy to administer. In fact, you can administer them to the whole class simply by dictating the words, which cuts down on time. Third, spelling inventories are research-based (Bear et al., 2020). There are also disadvantages. Students may have understandings of morphology but not be able to accurately spell words. Also, spelling inventories do not cover all the ways that researchers tend to assess morphology. For example, many assessments ask students to state the meanings of affixes or identify or dissect the morphemes in a word (e.g., Carlisle, 2000; Goodwin et al., 2021).

Spelling Inventories: Advantages and Disadvantages

- Are easy to administer
- Can be administered to the whole class
- Are not time-consuming to administer
- Spelling likely indicates mastery of a unit

- Gives only a "ballpark estimate"
- Are time-consuming to score
- Do not test for decoding
- Do not test for understanding of words

Morphological Assessments

In the primary grades, teachers are used to assessing children's knowledge by asking them to spell and decode words containing various patterns (e.g., short vowels, consonant clusters). But with morphemes, it is not just about spelling or decoding the word, but also understanding *meaning*—what the word's morphemes mean, how they add information or change the word in some way (e.g., from a verb to noun). It's also about deciphering a word's meaning from its morphemes.

Monster, P.I.

Monster, P.I., developed by researchers, allows you to assess students based on four morphology skills (Carlisle, 2000; Bowers et al., 2010; Goodwin et al., 2021; Henry, 2019):

1. Identifying morphemes in words

2. Identifying words' parts of speech based on their suffixes (e.g., *-ous* = adjective)

3. Identifying the meaning of words based on their morphemes (e.g., *bi level* = two levels)

4. Decoding and spelling complex words (e.g., *traction*, *intractable*, *retract*)

This assessment powerfully explains the reading and comprehension abilities of students in grades 5–8 (Goodwin et al., 2021). Although this assessment is not designed for students in grades K–4, I share it because it illustrates levels of morphological development (e.g., reading and spelling are harder than Odd Man Out) and because it is free and has a clever, engaging digital interface for students.

> ### Can identify units of meaning in a word (awareness)
>
> - **Odd Man Out** Which word is not related? a) define; b) deflate; and c) defrost (Answer: define)
> - **Meaning Puzzles** Which words are related? a) discredit; b) sacred; and c) incredible (Answer: discredit and incredible)
>
> ### Can use suffixes to gain or change syntactic info (parts of speech)
>
> - **Real-Word Suffix** The colonists _____ against the unfair taxes of the king. a) revolution; b) revolted; c) revolutionary (Answer: revolted)
> - **Making It Fit** The jacket provided _____. a) warm; b) warmth (Answer: warmth)
>
> ### Can use morphology to understand the meaning of a word
>
> - **Word Detectives** Students are given a sentence with a word and must figure out the word's meaning using the parts. For example, the teacher asked the students to form a semicircle (semi = half + circle).
>
> ### Can read and spell words with multiple morphemes
>
> - **Read** complex words
> - **Spell** complex words or identify the correct spelling

Monster, P.I. is gamified (so most children enjoy taking it), research-tested, and available online. The website (worddetectives.com) provides access to the assessment, along with directions for teachers about how the results can inform their teaching. The multidimensional elements of the assessment help teachers to see beyond decoding and spelling words to the layers of knowledge that students build as they acquire insight about meaningful language units. However, Monster, P.I. only covers morphemes and is designed for grades 5–8. It is not useful to primary-grade teachers working on first multisyllabic words, compounds, and inflectional morphemes.

Special Considerations When Assessing Morphology

Students come to school speaking a variety of languages and with a variety of dialects, which can impact their learning of big words. In this section, I address some considerations for assessment.

Multilingual Learners

The gift of multi-literacy presents students with remarkable opportunities, but also some challenges.

About 20 percent of U.S. students speak a home language other than English, and a large percentage of those students are bilingual Spanish speakers. According to Valdez-Pierce (2023), the closer the language is to English, the easier the acquisition of literacy in that language is. Because English is a Romance language, influenced by Latin, languages such as French and Spanish are similar, and, as discussed in Chapter 8, many Romance languages share words with the same roots. However, many students in schools do not speak Romance languages.

Valdez-Pierce also touches on the importance of assessing multilingual learners' literacy levels in their first language. When it comes to word-level instruction, there are several tools they can use, such as spelling inventories in Spanish that can determine a student's understanding of phoneme-graphemes and morphemes in the student's own language, including *Words Their Way with English Learners* (Helman et al., 2012) and *Core Phonics Survey* (Park et al., 2014). These assessments can help you understand whether students possess universal understandings of literacy that they can transfer to their English learning.

With respect to formal assessments, students often have difficulty simply accessing items because the language load of the directions is high. If you use the informal assessments described in this chapter, this may be less of a problem. But if an assessment does not have one, clear response type (e.g., read the word, spell the word), model *several* items to *show* students what to do.

You can also have students respond to the item informally, even orally, first in their home language and then in English. For example, if the item is defining the prefix *re-*, you might say, "What does the prefix *re-* mean? In Spanish you might say it as 'ray,' as in *releer*. Tell a friend what *re-* means in Spanish. Now tell a friend in English what *re-* means. Do you know an English word with *re-*?" You can use an online translation app to help you with any language you might need.

Another challenge is that items contain language that is decontextualized, which can strip multilingual learners of supports that they need to understand. Let's say you want to remind students of the context in which they learned that prefix *re-* before assessing them. You might say, "I want you to look at this anchor chart and remember the pictures that we drew for all of these different prefixes. Javier, do you remember the drawing you did for this prefix (points to *re-*)? What did you draw and why? Yes! You drew these arrows pointing round and round to each other. You even made these funny lightning bolts. You were trying to show that this prefix means what? Can you say it in Spanish first?"

Dialectical Differences

Dialects are the unique ways people in particular regions or from particular cultural groups use language (Wheeler et al., 2012). They reflect differences in which people say the sounds in words, use grammar (e.g., *y'all*, *ain't*, *He say*), use vocabulary (e.g., *pop* vs. *soda*), and, yes, use—or don't use—morphemes (e.g., *two apple*, *David table*). For example, in some regions of the south, people might say the word *pin* as "peen," or in Boston the word *car* might sound like "cah." All of those differences are rule-governed in speech communities that linguists increasingly suggest should not be viewed as degradations.

In some dialects, certain morphemes are not used or are used differently. When we are teaching and assessing students, we need to be sensitive to and respectful of their dialects. Many of the assessments described in this chapter require students to read or spell words. Researchers suggest an approach that draws on a code-switching model. In their book *Code-Switching Lessons:*

Grammar Strategies for Linguistically Diverse Writers, Rebecca Wheeler and Rachel Swords suggest explicitly teaching students to code switch between the language they use in formal settings (school, work) and informal settings (home, family gatherings). Cecilia M. Espinosa and Laura Ascenzi-Moreno (2021) suggest translanguaging, an approach in which students use their entire linguistic and sociocultural repertoires to develop their language and literacy skills.

In Closing, Remember...

Unlike measures for some areas of instruction, such as fluency or phonics, the measures for morphology are not quite as well developed. But these tips will help as you move forward.

- Assessment is the key to using a scope and sequence wisely. In Chapter 2, I discussed how a scope and sequence is like a road map for instruction. But a road map is no good if you don't know where you are. One of the purposes of assessment is to understand where students are so that you can start at the right place.
- Decoding and spelling inventories reveal the types of words that students can read and spell. These assessments contain carefully selected words that feature a variety of morphemes and syllable types.
- Morphology is about decoding and spelling words, but also knowing how word parts work. Morphological assessments address several skills, not simply the most advanced skills. Lower-level skills might include identifying morphemes in words, identifying words' parts of speech based on their suffixes, and identifying the meaning of words based on their morphemes.
- The most informative assessments of roots, prefixes, and derivational suffixes may be teacher-designed. Often teachers will create their own multidimensional assessments following a unit or root or derivational suffixes with questions that not only ask students to identify the meanings of morphemes, but also to show their understandings of how the parts work in sentences or authentic texts.

WHAT TO TEACH, WHEN TO TEACH IT, AND HOW TO TEACH IT

PART II

CHAPTER 4

Big Ideas on Teaching Big Words: Research-Based Principles

In Chapter 1, I covered several important points about *what to teach*: linguistic content such as such as syllables, morphemes, and the similarities and differences between them. In this chapter, I cover *how to teach* big words, focusing on broad ideas that work across most word parts. I've broken it into two sections. The first section describes "ingredients" that should be in place for students to learn big words. The second section identifies a series of research-based how-tos that you can start implementing tomorrow. Let's get started!

Four Ingredients for Successful Learning

To decode, understand, and spell big words successfully, students need a big-words mindset, a curiosity about words, the skills to crack them, and, of course, efficient, effective instruction.

A Big-Words Mindset

First, students need, what I call, a "big-words mindset." By that, I mean the confidence to try a big word, without being intimidated by it and shutting down. This mindset is important, and developing it must start in kindergarten. We simply cannot ignore complex words in grades K–2 and expect students to embrace them in grade 3 and above.

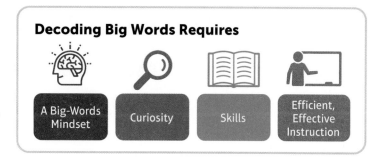

Decoding Big Words Requires

A Big-Words Mindset | Curiosity | Skills | Efficient, Effective Instruction

I saw this firsthand when Ishtar, one of my third graders, was reading a book about the solar system. She came to a sentence that said, "The sun is over 90 million miles away from Earth," and froze at the word *million*. She just stopped and then looked up at me.

"Give it a shot. Do you see parts?" I prodded.

"No. I can't do that word," she insisted.

And that was it. She was not going to try. In her mind, big words were just not something she could do. She did not have a big-words mindset.

Curiosity

Along with the will to at least *try* big words, students also must be curious about words. Let me illustrate with an example. I was reading Brian Doyle's book *Martin Marten*, a beautiful story about the interplay between man and nature, with a marten as the central character. Hmmm, did you just stop at my use of the word *marten*? Do you know that word, *marten*? I did not.

Now, another question—did that word cause you to pause and wonder, "What is a *marten*?" Did you pick up your phone and Google it? As an educator, I hope the answer is yes. After all, you're all about learning! Presumably, you love learning as much as teaching. You want to know. You are curious. That is what we want to foster in students—a sense of excitement, inquiry, and empowerment around words—the drive to know about them.

Learning about words is fascinating and, as we keep reading books, articles, and websites, we will constantly meet ones we do not know. I've recently met *oleaginous*, *sentential*, *prodromal*, and *dipsomaniac*. Being a reader myself and reading widely, including non-professional materials, is essential to fostering a big-words mindset and curiosity in young learners. When I read, I experience what *they* experience, and it helps me reach them. (I also read because it takes me out of my professional world, and it expands and enriches my life. It's a mini-vacation!)

The best approaches to teaching big words send students on word excursions: What are some of the words that have the root *tract* in them (e.g., *detract*, *subtract*, *intractable*, *contract*)? How does the meaning of *tract* (pull, drag) relate to the word *contract*? Are the bases of *display* and *playful* related? Students will apply that curiosity in their writing as well—I want to write *hoping*, but how do I add *-ing*?

Skills

Of course, being willing to attempt big words and being curious about them is not enough. When students do not have the *skills* to unpack complex words—to understand, decode, and spell them—the balloon bursts. That is where instruction comes in. To get to the word *million*, Ishtar needed to know the *-ion* ending, the consonant *m* and short *i* sound, and the prefix *mill-*.

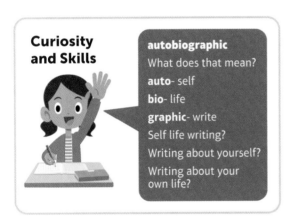

Curiosity and Skills

autobiographic
What does that mean?
auto- self
bio- life
graphic- write
Self life writing?
Writing about yourself?
Writing about your own life?

Readers who attempt and successfully read big words and can build and write big words know a lot. They know how word parts work. For example, they know the conventions for adding inflections. They know if three words share the same morpheme, their spellings may look the same, but may not sound the same (e.g., *electric*, *electricity*, *electrical*). They know the meanings of prefixes and suffixes.

Most importantly, they know how to problem-solve while reading when you are not nearby. The combination of a big-words mindset, curiosity, and skills grows into a beautiful self-sustaining process, the kind that prompts a student to stop when he or she is reading a book about frogs or question what *cumulus clouds* are in a passage about weather.

Efficient, Effective Instruction

Instruction is where it starts. When we teach efficiently and effectively, we develop students' skills, mindsets, and curiosities about words. Instruction in multisyllabic, multimorphemic words is not exactly like phonics. Yes, it includes teaching students to convert graphemes into words or syllables, but also to think about the structure of words and the meaning in that structure.

"I am just not comfortable with this stuff," explained Maria Elena, a teacher in Oregon. "I can teach a kid letters and sounds, and show them how to blend them into words. But when it comes to big words, my tool kit is empty. It's like I have a hammer and screwdriver for sounding out words, but when kids get to a long word, those tools often don't work. It's like I need a drill, wrench, and saw to do my job." The emphasis on phonics in preservice and in-service teacher education has eclipsed high-quality preparation in helping students handle the kinds of words they will see in texts above the most basic levels.

How to Teach Big Words: Research-Based Principles

In this section, I identify some principles that inform the teaching of big words.

Teach Students How Morphemes Work

If you're used to teaching phonics, taking the next step to teaching decoding and understanding morphemes can be huge. Most of us are not used to asking students to integrate sound units with meaning units. The work of decoding simple phoneme/grapheme relationships is different from the work that includes morphemes. When we ask students to think about words morphemically, we ask them to go a step further, to not only sound out parts but to also understand the meaning and function of those parts. For

Decoding Graphemes Into Phonemes

The <u>cat</u> played on the rug.

cat		
	phoneme/grapheme	morpheme
cat	/k/ /æ/ /t/	cat
cat = furry, four-legged, feline animal		

Decoding Graphemes Into Phonemes and *Then Into Morphemes*

The directions were <u>unreadable</u>.

unreadable		
	phoneme/grapheme	morpheme
un	/u/ /n/ = "un"	un (prefix) = "not"
read	/r/ /e/ /d/ = "read"	read (base) = "decode print"
able	/ə/ /b/ /l/ = "able"	able (suffix) = "something that one can do"; turns word into adjective
un + read + able, "unreadable" = something that is not readable		

example, decoding the word *unreadable* requires sounding out its parts, but also to put those parts together to extract a meaning.

Notice that one part, a prefix (*un-*), changes the meaning, and another part, a derivational suffix (*able*), converts the verb *read* into an adjective meaning "something that one can do." When students apply morphology, they balance the code and the meaning of the code. They do a code-related activity and a meaning-related activity all at once.

Provide Explicit Instruction *and* Lots of Application Opportunities

When I talk to teachers, I often find disagreement about teaching words in isolation and teaching them in context. I encounter teachers who will say, "You have to look at words in isolation to really understand how they work. Kids can't learn this stuff on the fly while reading a text. That leads to gaps." And I encounter teachers who are frustrated by being required to teach lengthy lessons on words alone: "We are being required to spend so much time on lessons on isolated words that the kids barely get a chance to read and write."

Both responses are valid—you can't learn about words without analyzing them in isolation, but who cares if students can analyze words if they don't use them to read and write extended text? They must have explicit instruction and lots of application opportunities.

High-quality instruction in word parts means teaching, explicitly and clearly, the meanings of parts, the conventions of adding parts, and many other aspects of language. For example, let's say a teacher is working on the prefix, *dis-*. Explicit instruction might sound like this:

Today we are going to learn about the prefix dis-.

A prefix is a word part that we put on the front of a word that changes the word's meaning. [Shows prefix card.]

> dis

Can someone sound out this prefix? It is a closed syllable. Yes, dis- *with a short vowel. This prefix,* dis-, *means "not." When I put it on the front of a word it changes the word to mean "not"_____. Not ...* [Shows base word card.]

Here is a base word. Can someone read this word? It has a vowel team syllable type at the ending and the first sound is schwa. Yes, it is agree.

> agree

Now, watch as I put the prefix dis- *in front of* agree *and make a new word:* disagree.

dis | agree

Now I can tell what the word means too. dis- *means* not, *so* not agree. Disagree *means "not agree."*

Now let's read more words with the prefix dis- *in them.*

While explicit instruction is essential, it is often misinterpreted—some teachers think it prohibits applied practice in reading and understanding words in authentic texts. Nothing could be further from the truth. Students *must* apply their knowledge of word parts to actual reading and writing. Encourage students to do the following:

- Read books, articles, and web pages with big words.
- Write using big words.
- Keep a log of words from their reading that contain parts they know.
- Keep a list of prefixes, suffixes, and roots, and their meanings.
- Discuss words in small groups.

Tap into the power of having students *talk* about words. Too often schoolwork has students working silently in isolation with a pencil in hand. Talking about words is helpful for students, as long as we provide clarification and direction when they need it. To show you what I mean, the short vignette below

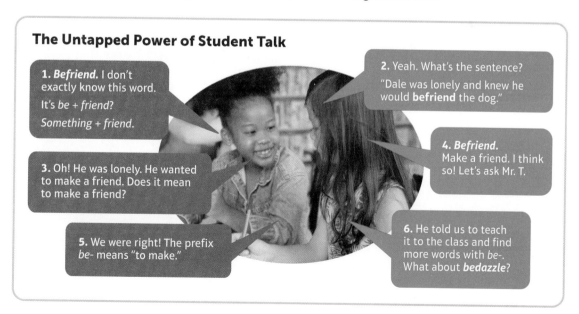

The Untapped Power of Student Talk

1. *Befriend.* I don't exactly know this word. It's *be + friend? Something + friend.*

2. Yeah. What's the sentence? "Dale was lonely and knew he would **befriend** the dog."

3. Oh! He was lonely. He wanted to make a friend. Does it mean to make a friend?

4. *Befriend.* Make a friend. I think so! Let's ask Mr. T.

5. We were right! The prefix *be-* means "to make."

6. He told us to teach it to the class and find more words with *be-*. What about **bedazzle**?

captures two fourth graders trying to figure out the less common prefix *be-* (e.g., *belittle, befriend, bedraggle, befit*).

Teach Students to Find the Base Word

When they talk about big-words instruction, many educators—me included—tend to focus on word parts (e.g., *-ing, -es, -ify*) more than base words (e.g., *walk-ing, box-es, glori-fy*) or Latin and Greek roots (e.g., *ject*—to throw). That is only half of the picture (Bowers et al., 2010). We need to help students understand the concept, from the start, that words fall into three categories: 1) a base word (e.g., *nag, purple, vibrate*); 2) base + bound morpheme (e.g., *nagged, pretreating*), or 3) Latin or Greek root + bound morpheme (e.g., *structure*).

Remember, these terms:

- **base word:** a stand-alone word to which bound morphemes are added
- **bound morpheme:** a word part that adds meaning, but cannot stand alone (e.g., *pre-, -ing, -ment, -ful, -s*)
- **Latin or Greek root:** a word part that is central to a word's definition, but cannot stand alone (e.g., *aud > auditorium, tele > telephone*)

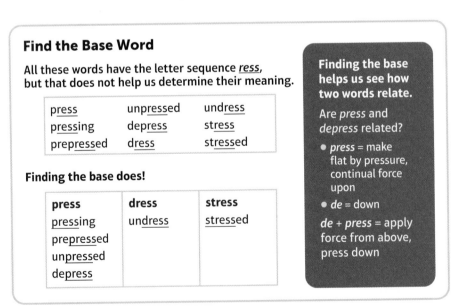

Find the Base Word

All these words have the letter sequence *ress*, but that does not help us determine their meaning.

press	unpressed	undress
pressing	depress	stress
prepressed	dress	stressed

Finding the base does!

press	dress	stress
pressing	undress	stressed
prepressed		
unpressed		
depress		

Finding the base helps us see how two words relate.

Are *press* and *depress* related?

- *press* = make flat by pressure, continual force upon
- *de* = down

de + *press* = apply force from above, press down

Understanding big words often starts with identifying a word's base—the meaningful core of the word, which is different from identifying its letter sequences or even one of its sound parts. In the example above, all the words have the sequence -ress, but different bases. The best way to teach students is by having them first spot the meaningful core, the base word, and then solve how the prefixes and suffixes add meaning. When students do that, they begin to understand how words relate to one another, and that is HUGE! When we store words in the brain, those words connect and form relationships in networks. So building *relationships* among words through instructions gives students a leg up (Willingham, 2017).

As early as kindergarten, we should be using the language of base words. Building awareness that words usually do not work solo helps students develop a big-words mindset. Here is how instruction might sound in the early grades:

- "Oh look, this word *vans* has the base word *van* and then a part *s* to tell us there is more than one van. Can you find the base word in *pigs*?"
- "Wow! This is a compound word (*classroom*). It has two base words. What are they? Yes! *Class* and *room*. This is a room for a class."
- "This might be a little tricky. This word (*hoping*) might look like it has *hop*, but that is not the base word. Think about what happens when you add -*ing*."
- "Let's think about that word *definition*. What is the base word? Remember sometimes vowels change when we add endings. Yes! It is *define*, but that's not what we hear, is it? We hear *defin-* with a short *i* when we make it *definition*."

Teach Students to Think About Spelling and Meaning From the Start

Ever wonder why young readers produce spellings such as *dogz*, *walkt*, or *fotograf*? It's largely because they tend to crack words phonetically, meaning they think only about the letter sounds they hear, because that is what we are teaching them, sound spellings. This may be due to their development and the ways that we are teaching literacy.

When students begin to learn about morphemes, they approach words differently because English spellings prioritize *structure* (visual spellings) over *consistent sound*. For example, we use -*ed* to spell the past tense but that same pattern could have different sounds: /t/ (e.g., *asked*), /d/ (e.g., *spilled*), or /ed/ (e.g., *painted*). We spell the Greek root *photo* with the Greek spelling *ph* for /f/ to show how all words containing are part of a family.

Yes, one of the big milestones of early reading is mastering the alphabetic principle, but that gets children only so far. English is morphophonemic, and they must interpret the letter-sound units from a meaning perspective as well. In other words, we must also teach the morphological principle!

In English, words related in meaning are related in *spelling* even if there are shifts in the sounds that we pronounce (Bear et al., 2020). Related words are

The Morphological Principle: The Second Principle of English Spelling

In English, the first principle that operates as we spell, decode, and find meaning in words is the alphabetic principle—the fact that visual symbols (letters) represent speech sounds (phonemes).

The second principle is the morphological principle, which teachers don't explain to students enough—the fact that morphemes, or meaningful word parts, are spelled consistently across related words, even when their pronunciations are different. We see this in the primary grades with, for example, the three sounds of -*ed* (e.g., *heated* /ed/, *combed* /d/, *mopped* /t/), and it ramps up in intermediate grades, when students are learning longer words. Take, for example, the root *duc*, where the vowel and final letter are may be pronounced differently, depending on the word—*educate, reduce, conduct*. Why don't we spell *educate* with a *k (edukate)*? Or *reduce* with an *s (reduse)*? We spell those words with *duc* because they are related to the root *duc/duct* and, therefore, are spelled with the same letters, even though the sounds that we hear when we say them are different.

Think about it. The morphological principle is hard for kids because it is a bit of a reversal of the alphabetic principle, which tells them, "When you hear a sound, select the correct letters to spell the sound." But for decoding longer words, the morphological principle says, "When you decode or spell a word, use sounds *but also* think about a related word to spell it."

- Words related in meaning are often related in spelling, even if sounds shift when we pronounce them (Bear et al., 2020).

  sign > signature > signal

- English prioritizes consistent spelling of morphemes over consistent pronunciation of them (Bear et al., 2020).

Uncertain about how to spell a word?

epesodic? epasodic? episodic?

Think about a related word:

episode!

There's an *i* in the middle.

episodic

spelled the same even if the sound is not maintained. We used visual spellings to maintain meaning connections between words (Chomsky, 1970). For example, the first part of the words *electric*, *electrical*, and *electricity* all are spelled the same way with a *c* in the last syllable, even though sound changes. The *c* in *electric* and *electrical* sounds like /k/ but the c in *electricity* sounds like /s/. Here's another example:

> Did you know the letter *s* spells the /z/ sound more than it spells the /s/ sound? We typically teach students that the letter *s* spells /s/ and that when it spells /z/ it's an exception, but that is not true! We use the letter *s* to pluralize nouns or show verb tenses. Whether we hear the /z/ sound at the end of a plural word or a singular, present tense word, we see the letter *s*. When we spell in English we maintain visual consistency of *s* over the phonetic consistency of the sound /s/.

Younger students often default to phonetic similarity when determining if two words are related (Derwing, 1976). For example, they may decide that *interest* and *invisible* are related because they both share *in*. The prefix *pre-* in *predict* means "before" as in "to tell before" but the *pre-* in *pretty* does not mean before, because it is not a prefix in that word.

To determine if two words are related, encourage students to first check if the words' spellings (structure) are similar. If they are, then have students take the words apart and determine if the units share the same meaning. For example, does the *un-* in *under* and *undo* work the same way?

Keep Instruction Active and Multifaceted

During effective, research-based word instruction, students working with parts do two things: 1) build words up and 2) take words apart. I call it the LEGOs® principle: As students construct and deconstruct words, they learn how parts fit together (Beck & Beck, 2013; Goodwin et al., 2012; Kieffer & Lesaux, 2007; Toste et al., 2017, 2019). Just as students who play with LEGOs learn that a 1 x 2 block cannot support the weight of five 2 x 4 blocks, students will learn that adding *-ing* to a CVC word requires doubling the final consonants (e.g., *napping*, *sitting*, *begging*). Think about my LEGOs principle as "word engineering," or understanding how parts fit.

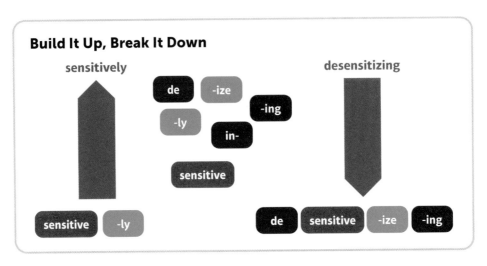

Build It Up, Break It Down

Researchers Toste and colleagues had students identify word parts, put those parts together to make words, and then take the words apart (2019). Specifically, here's what the students did:

1. **Reviewed vowel patterns** To read long words, students must be able to read base words and roots using basic decoding skills. Thus, they practiced letter sounds in isolation, in real words, and in pseudo words for the many vowel graphemes in English.

2. **Practiced high-frequency affixes** Students practiced reading common prefixes and suffixes in isolated format (e.g., *de-*, *dis-*, *-ing*, *-ed*).

3. **Blended word parts** Students received words in parts (e.g., *re-run-ning*) and blended the parts together.

4. **Isolated affixes in words, while being timed** Students identified and circled prefixes and suffixes in full words. They were timed, which built fluency and automatic recognition of parts.

5. **Wrote words with affixes** Students wrote dictated affixed words to practice encoding word parts.

6. **Practiced fluent reading** Students practiced timed reading of words containing a variety of part types. Then the researchers asked them to read a list of words for 30 seconds and noted the words they could decode.

7. **Practiced reading increasingly complex texts** Early in the intervention, students read sentences with the choral-read, echo-read, or whisper-read. Later they read connected texts.

In the study, students who participated in these building-up and breaking-down activities with word parts did better on word decoding and passage comprehension.

Use a Problem-Solving Approach

The research-based ideas for teaching big words that I've suggested thus far require problem-solving (Kieffer & Lesaux, 2007; Goodwin et al., 2012, 2013; Lovett et al., 2000; Toste et al., 2017, 2019). When students hit a big word while reading, they problem-solve by looking for meaningful parts they know. Lovett and colleagues call this technique SPY for Seek the Parts You Know (2000).

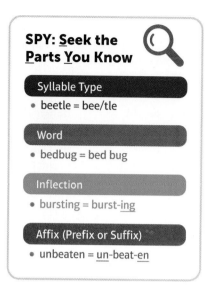

SPY: Seek the Parts You Know

Syllable Type
- beetle = bee/tle

Word
- bedbug = bed bug

Inflection
- bursting = burst-ing

Affix (Prefix or Suffix)
- unbeaten = un-beat-en

(Lovett et al., 2000)

The beauty of SPY is that it is flexible. Students approach a big word by breaking it down and looking for *any* part(s) they know. If they know -*ing*, for example, they can use that knowledge to read and understand words such as *playing* and *amazingly*. If they are more advanced and know a Greek root such as *scope*, they can use that knowledge to read and spell words such as *telescope* and *microscopic*. SPY even works with syllable types (e.g., *ta-ble* = open syllable + consonant -*le*). It also builds a big-words mindset by giving students a basic way to dive into a hard word. Lastly, SPY is a great formative assessment. For example, if I say to a student, "What do you SPY in this word (*beetle*)?" and she says "bee" but misses the consonant -*le* syllable type, I know she needs work with that syllable type. A word of caution, though: If students have not been taught about meaningful word parts, SPY will not get them very far.

Baumann and colleagues developed a similar problem-solving strategy, PQRST, working with fifth graders (2003). When students encounter a big word, they identify the prefix and its meaning (P), the "Queen Root" and its meaning (because the root is the "queen" of the word), and then the suffix and its meaning (S). After identifying those parts, students put the total word together (T) and describes its meaning. (Read more about this in Chapter 7.)

Capitalize on Cognates

Many teachers work with students who speak a language other than English at home, which can present wonderful big-word learning opportunities. In the United States, many of those students are Spanish/English speakers—

What Are Cognates?

Cognates are words from different languages that share similar spellings, meanings, and perhaps pronunciations.

English	Italian
air	aria
fresh	fresca
respond	rispondo

English	Spanish
information	información
police	policía
opportunity	oportunidad

English	German
book	buch
finger	finger
guest	gast

and many words in English and Spanish are cognates, words with a similar spelling, pronunciation, and meaning in both languages. Those similarities arise because those cognates come from the same roots. In Chapter 2, I described how English is a Germanic language that has been heavily influenced by Latin, as Spanish has. For example, *hospital,* a Spanish word, and *hospital*, the English version, look and mean the same thing, but have pronunciation differences. Occasionally there are *false cognates*, words that sound and/or look alike, but do not share the same meaning. For example, *rope* and *ropa* look and sound the same, but do not mean the same thing. That said, about 90 percent of English/Spanish cognates *do* mean the same thing, which is why teaching them is a good use of our instructional time.

In Closing, Remember...

There are four essential ingredients to learning big words: the right mindset, curiosity, skills, and high-quality instruction, and seven research-based big ideas that apply to teaching big words:

- Teach students how morphemes work
- Provide explicit instruction and lots of application opportunities
- Get students into the habit of finding the base word
- Encourage students to think about spelling and meaning from the start
- Keep instruction active and multifaceted
- Use a problem-solving approach
- Capitalize on cognates for multilingual learners

I hope this chapter got you excited about teaching big words, and that you can see yourself using my suggestions with your students. In the remaining chapters, I provide strategies for teaching specific types of word parts.

Compounds, Contractions, and Inflections Without Spelling Changes in Grades K–1

As I've mentioned, there has been a trend in K–1 phonics to concentrate almost exclusively on decoding single-syllable words, to the exclusion of words with multiple syllables and morphemes. It seems almost every teaching blog post, video, and tip about decoding focuses on single-syllable words. There are posts, videos, and tips on how to blend words, how to teach the nasalized *a*, how to enunciate phonemes without the added schwa, and how to teach the mouth moves for letter sounds. Of course, being able to decode single-syllable words is a milestone skill that children need to decode words with multiple syllables and morphemes. The problem is many teachers breathe a big sigh of relief once that happens, as if their decoding work is done. But that's like declaring victory at the 2K mark of a 5K race—it's premature.

Even as early as kindergarten, students will encounter simple inflections (e.g., *-s*, *-ing*) or compound words (e.g., *backpack*), and we can teach them how to handle these words. By doing so, we are building their capacity for future reading by setting up a big-words mindset—a courage and confidence to read big words and not freeze. We are also setting up two important concepts:

1. Words have meaningful parts that can be added to them (bound morphemes) but cannot stand on their own (e.g., *-ed, -s, -ly, pre-*).

2. Every word can be a base word, a word onto which other parts can be added (e.g., *run, runn-ing, re-run, runn-er*).

Now, while I would not use the term *bound morpheme* with students, I would use *base word*. By teaching those basic ideas early on, they will not feel so strange in third grade.

What to Teach: Compounds, Contractions, and Inflections Without Spelling Changes

Compounds

The word *compound* literally means "to put together." Compound words are simply two base words that are put together, with **no** spelling changes to either one (e.g., *dog + house = doghouse*). If you want to know if a word is a compound, ask yourself, "Can each word stand alone as a base?" If so, it's a compound word or, as linguists call it, a root compound.

Compounds are an easy step into multisyllabic, multimorphemic words because the parts are recognizable, and they lay a foundation for finding base words in words with more complicated prefixes and suffixes later. Moreover, decoding them is usually not difficult. If students can read the words *night* and *light,* then, with a little instruction and a big-words mindset, they can read *nightlight*.

Compound words can be nouns (e.g., *baseball*), verbs (e.g., *skateboarding*), adjectives (e.g., *left-handed*), and prepositions (e.g., *inside*). There are three types of compound words:

Is It a Compound Word?

 haircut

Can *each* part of the word stand alone?
- *hair*? yes!
- *cut*? yes!

It's a compound word.

 precut

Can *each* part of the word stand alone?
- *pre*? no!
- *cut*? yes!

It's not a compound word!

1) closed (e.g., *rainbow*), 2) open (e.g., *ice cream*), and 3) hyphenated (e.g., *merry-go-round*). In elementary school, we typically focus on closed compound words. Although children will encounter all three types, I believe teaching hyphenated compound words in the primary grades should be reserved for students who would benefit from an additional challenge.

A *decodable compound* is a word in which *both* base words contain patterns that the student has been taught. We can teach decodable compound words throughout K–1. (See Appendix A: Decodable Compound Words Grouped by Pattern.)

Decodable Compounds

If students know	then they can decode
CVC • *sun, bed, tan, bug*	**CVC** • *bedbug, suntan*
Blends • *spot, hand*	**Blends in the Middle** • *sunspot, handset*
Digraphs, Blends, Digraph Blends • *back, fish, hand, lunch*	**Digraphs, Blends, Digraph Blends** • *backhand, sunfish, lunchbox*
Vowel Teams or *r*-Controlled • *air, load, car*	**Vowel Teams or *r*-Controlled** • *airlift, bypass, carload*

Facts About Compound Words

- *Compound* means to put together.
- Two complete base words that are joined together to make another word: *blueberry, baseball, birdhouse, cannot, within*
- There are no changes in the spellings of the base words.
- Compound words can be nouns, verbs, adjectives, adverbs, and prepositions.

- There are three types:
  1. **Closed** (words joined without space between them): *upshot, doghouse*
  2. **Open** (words with a space between them): *ice cream, cell phone, first aid, high school*
  3. **Hyphenated** (words joined by hyphen): *check-in, sister-in-law, empty-handed*

Contractions

The word *contract* means to draw together or make smaller. Contractions are common word pairs that are drawn together and made smaller using an apostrophe (e.g., *is not > isn't, he will > he'll, could have > could've, I would > I'd*). In most contractions, only one to two letters are replaced by the apostrophe. Start by teaching contractions in which the apostrophe replaces a single letter (e.g., *isn't, he's*). From there, move to those in which the apostrophe replaces two letters (e.g., *they'll, we'll*)—and, from there, those in which the apostrophe replaces three or more letters (e.g., *that would > that'd, who would, who had > who'd*).

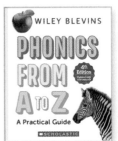

This list from Wiley Blevins's *Phonics From A to Z: A Practical Guide, Fourth Edition* (2023) contains common contractions for primary grades.

Contractions

am	have	not	us
I'm	I've	aren't	let's
	might've	can't	
are	should've	couldn't	**will**
they're	they've	didn't	I'll
we're	we've	doesn't	it'll
you're	would've	don't	he'll
	you've	hadn't	she'll
would		hasn't	that'll
I'd	**is**	haven't	they'll
it'd	here's	isn't	we'll
she'd	he's	mustn't	you'll
there'd	it's	needn't	
they'd	she's	shouldn't	
we'd	that's	wouldn't	
you'd	there's		
	what's		
	where's		
	who's		

(Blevins, 2023)

As with inflections, introduce the easier, most frequent contractions first, which are those that require the fewest letters to be removed, and move onto more challenging, less frequent ones from there:

1. Contractions with -s (e.g., *he's, it's*)

2. Contractions with *will* (e.g., *she'll, we'll*)

3. Contractions with *not* (e.g., *haven't, didn't*) + Contractions with *would/could/should* and *have* (e.g., *they've, she'd*)

Facts About Contractions

- *Contract* means to make smaller.
- The word *contraction* comes from Latin: *com* (with, together) + *tract* (to pull) = "to pull together"

- Contractions are two words combined. We create them by removing letters and replacing them with an apostrophe:

  is not = isn't
  should have = *should've*

Inflections Without Spelling Changes

Here's a passage from a book I was reading the other day: "As he came closer, he spoke with a slight inflection in his voice." The word *inflect* means to change slightly or alter. If you inflect your voice, you change or alter it. So, it stands to reason that inflections are word parts that we add to the ends of base words—nouns, verbs, or adjectives—that change or slightly alter them grammatically. As you can see in the chart on the next page, inflections add grammatical information related to number, verb tense (past, present), and comparisons. Inflections do not change the part of speech of a word—a noun remains a noun (e.g., *heart, hearts*), a verb remains a verb (e.g., *play, plays, playing*), and an adjective remains an adjective (e.g., *happy, happier, happiest*).

I remember how inflections work by thinking back to an inflected voice: An inflected voice is still saying the same thing just slightly differently; an inflected word is still saying the same thing only slightly changing it. In one analysis of elementary reading textbooks, researchers found that just three suffixes (-*s/-es*, -*ing*, and -*ed*), all of them inflections, accounted for 64 percent of words that had some type of affix. This suggests that we must teach a collection of simple inflections as soon as possible.

Inflection	Purpose	Added to	Examples
-s, -es, -ies	Plural	Noun	ships, bags
-s, -es, -ies	Tense Third Person Singular	Verb	[she, he, it]: runs, gets, sings
-ed	Past Tense	Verb	walked, parted
-en	Perfect Aspect	Verb	written, bitten
-ing	Progressive (Happening Now)	Verb	testing, munching
-er	Comparative	Adjective	tall, taller, tallest
-est	Superlative	Adjective	green, greener, greenest

When we add inflections to words, the spelling of the base word may change depending on how the word ends. The following are some examples:

- Double final consonant: *hop > hopping, hopped*
- Change *y* to *i*: *puppy > puppies, happy > happiest*
- Drop silent *e*: *name > naming, named*

In kindergarten and first grade, I recommend teaching inflections *without* spelling changes with one exception—drop the final *e*, because it is not complicated. In Chapter 7, where I explore teaching with prefixes and suffixes in depth, I address inflections with spelling changes. If you are teaching first grade and find your students ready to handle spelling changes, teach it.

I want to make a quick clarification about terms. Many teachers use the term *suffix* when they are talking about morphemes added to the end of words, but they do not differentiate between inflections and derivational suffixes. There is a difference, and it matters for teaching. Although derivational suffixes will be addressed more in Chapter 7, I want to provide a quick comparison between these two suffix types to help you understand why inflections come earlier in the scope and sequence. Inflections do add grammatical information but, in English, there are fewer of them. For this reason, inflections tend to be taught earlier and mastered. In contrast, derivational suffixes *do* change a word's part of speech, for example:

- A noun becomes a verb—e.g., *-ize, terror* (n) > *terrorize* (v)
- A noun becomes an adjective—e.g., *-al, music* (n) > *musical* (adj)
- An adjective becomes an adverb—e.g.,*-ly, quick* (adj) > *quickly*

Also, there are *more* derivational suffixes and students do not tend to develop insight about these until third grade. For that reason, derivational suffixes are usually taught in the secondary grades and beyond. One last point: I occasionally use the term "inflectional suffix" as a reminder that an inflection is a specific type of suffix.

-er Is a Derivational and Inflectional Suffix

Inflectional Suffix	Derivational Suffix
• Comparative	• "One who"
• Does *not* change part of speech:	• Does change part of speech:
- big, bigger, biggest	-batter
- tall, taller, tallest	-driver
- nice, nicer, nicest	-puncher
- green, greener, greenest	-toaster
- happy, happier, happiest	

Facts About Inflections

- *Inflect* means to change, alter, or modify.
- An inflection is a form of suffix.
- It is a morpheme added to a base word that may be a noun, verb, or adjective.
- It expresses grammatical information:

  -s   *animals* (more than one)
  -ing *pitching* (happening now)
  -s   *runs* (third-person singular)
  -ed *helped* (past tense)
  -est *happiest* (comparative-most)

- It modifies a word without changing its part of speech.

  Animal is still a noun when an *s* is added.

  Pitch is still a verb when *-ing* is added.

  Happy is still an adjective when the *y* is dropped and *-iest* is added.

When to Teach It

Broad Scope and Sequence

There are three main types of big words that young readers should encounter right from the start: 1) decodable compounds, 2) contractions, and 3) inflections without spelling changes.

Contractions are typically taught in first grade, but compound words and inflections are not. Yet, they can be! Even kindergartners can put together two decodable words to make a compound (e.g., *catnap*, *bedbug*). In both kindergarten and first grade, students can also handle adding inflections to words where there are no spelling changes.

In the next section, I explain how to interweave those three types of big words into a typical phonics scope and sequence.

Adding Compounds, Contractions, and Inflections Without Spelling Changes Into a Typical K–2 Phonics Curriculum

In the chart below, the **green** rows contain patterns typically taught in K–2 phonics. The **blue** rows contain big-words add-ins. For example, after teaching short vowel/CVC words, add in 1) inflections: add -*s* (no spelling change), 2) decodable compounds with CVC, and 3) syllable type label: closed (CVC) and open.

Major Patterns Taught in K–2 Phonics	Example Words
Consonants and Short Vowels	
Short Vowel/CVC Words	hat, hit, net, top
Inflections: add -*s* (no spelling change)	hats, hits, nets, tops
Decodable compounds with CVC	catnap, bedbug
Syllable types: Closed (CVC) and Open (Ch. 6)	go/got, no/not, so/sob
Contractions with '*s*	she's, he's, it's
Blends and Digraphs	trust, munch, test, fish
Decodable compounds with CCVC, CVCC, CVCCC	handbag, uplift, lunchbox
Inflections: -*ed*, -*ing*, -*er* (no spelling change)	trusted, munched, fishing
Syllable type: Closed (CVCC) or (CVCCC) (Ch. 6)	bent, trust, dish, munch
Contractions with '*ll*	he'll, they'll
Silent *e*	hike, tape, hope
Inflections: -*s*, -*ing*, -*er*, -*ed* (no change -*s*, drop -*e*)	hikes, hiked, hiking, nicer
Decodable compounds	baseline, icepick, timeline
Syllable type: Silent *e* (Ch. 6)	bat/bate, cap/cape
Vowel Teams	boat, seat, toil, shout
Inflections -*e*, -*er*, -*ed*, -*s* (no spelling change)	greener, teams, seated, toiling
Syllable type: Vowel Team (Ch. 6)	point, roast, peak
Contractions with *n't*	can't, isn't, would've, couldn't
***r*-controlled Vowels**	bark, tore, first, term, turn
Inflections: -*er*, -*er*, -*ed*, -*s* (no spelling change)	barks, barked, barking, termed, harder
Syllable type: *r*-Controlled Vowel (Ch. 6)	hut/hurt, back/bark
Syllable type: Consonant -*le* (See Ch. 6)	trickle, puzzle, brittle
Review all syllable types and words with a mix of types (See Ch. 6)	beetle, peacemaker, corner

This chart shows how decodable compounds, contractions, and inflections without spelling changes can be added to a typical K–2 phonics curriculum. You will notice that syllable types are interwoven into the chart, but not covered until Chapter 6. I've included them to give you a bird's-eye view of all the big-words content in early phonics.

Add in Decodable Compounds

As they are learning how to decode single-syllable words, students also handle decodable compounds. Putting together two words that have patterns you know and can blend is not a vertical skill—one that represents something new or different. After a five- to six-week unit on short vowels (e.g., *sun*, *tan*, *bed*, *bug*), students can be taught compounds with the CVC pattern (e.g., *suntan*). However, don't try to teach compounds before students have mastered the single-syllable pattern. Instruction will be overwhelming and fall apart. Teaching decodable compounds should come *after* students can automatically and easily blend the pattern (e.g., *sun*), not when decoding is effortful and requires multiple attempts: "sssuuuun, ssssuun, ssun, sun." (See Appendix A: Decodable Compound Words Grouped by Pattern.)

Add in Contractions

Most first-grade curricula do include contractions, and they are taught throughout the year, based on the frequency of the contraction and its difficulty, which is based on the number of letters removed or represented by the apostrophe (e.g., *isn't* = one letter removed, *should've* = two letters removed). I suggest the following order:

1. Contractions with -*s* (e.g., *he's*, *it's*)
2. Contractions with *will* (e.g., *she'll*, *we'll*)
3. Contractions with *not* (e.g., *haven't*, *didn't*)
4. Contractions with *would*, *could*, *should*, and *have* (e.g., *they've*, *she'd*)

I have interspersed them throughout this scope and sequence in a similar way, beginning with the contractions with -*s*, followed by those with *will* and then those with *not* and *would*, *should*, or *could*.

Add in Inflections Without Spelling Changes

The third add-in to early phonics instruction is common inflections that do not require spelling changes, such as -*s*, -*ing*, -*ed* (e.g., *fishing*, *runs*, *tested*). As you teach these four target decoding skills, add in inflections without spelling changes, like the following:

1. **Add in -*s* to short vowel (CVC) words as they are learned.** We can show young readers how to add -*s* as soon as kindergarten because adding an -*s* to the end of a CVC word requires no spelling changes.

2. **Add in -*er*, -*ed*, -*ing* to words ending in blends or digraphs (e.g., *munch*, *fish*, *test*, *bend*, *stack*).**

3. **Add in -*er*, -*ed*, -*ing* to words with vowel teams (e.g., *toot*, *play*, *steam*, *moan*).**

4. **Add in -*er*, -*ed*, -*ing* to r-controlled words (e.g., *park*, *lurk*, *point*, *herd*).** When adding -*er*, -*ed*, -*ing* to a word with digraphs and blends at the end, vowel teams, and *r*-controlled vowels, there are also no spelling changes in most words.

How to Teach It: Compounds

Here are research-based, classroom-tested activities for teaching compounds.

A Routine for Teaching Compounds

Compounds are typically the first words that students encounter. Decoding them builds students' capacity for finding base words in the future, as well as their confidence to tackle big words. This straightforward five-step routine is described below. When choosing examples, make sure students can read all the patterns in both words in the compound. The list of decodable compounds in Appendix A will help you choose words.

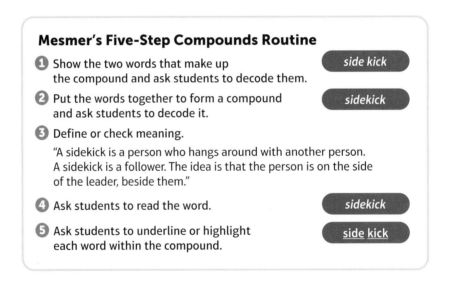

Mesmer's Five-Step Compounds Routine

1. Show the two words that make up the compound and ask students to decode them.   `side kick`

2. Put the words together to form a compound and ask students to decode it.   `sidekick`

3. Define or check meaning.
   "A sidekick is a person who hangs around with another person. A sidekick is a follower. The idea is that the person is on the side of the leader, beside them."

4. Ask students to read the word.   `sidekick`

5. Ask students to underline or highlight each word within the compound.   `side kick`

Define Compounds

When I first started teaching compounds, I did not ask students to define them. I thought the meanings were obvious but then I realized that to many students, they are not! Even if the compound was seemingly transparent, my students could often decode it, but did not have experience or context to understand it. For example, they might have been able to understand that *blueberry* means a berry that is blue, but may not know that it's small and sweet and used to make all kinds of delicious desserts.

I always give students a quick definition after they read compounds to build their vocabulary. Some compounds form entirely new concepts, people, places, or things. For example, *takeoff* refers to the action of an airplane lifting into the air and relates to air travel concepts. We don't use that phrase as a compound in all circumstances, such as when we say, "She is going to *take off* her coat." The point is that big words and their parts are usually connected to meaning. We want students to get that idea right away.

Check the Meaning

Compound with **transparent** meaning	Compound with **some connection**	Compound with a **completely new meaning**
The two words come together to make a word that closely reflects each word's meaning.	The two words come together to make a word that connects to each word's meaning, but not exactly.	The two words come together to form a word that is completely different.
blueberry = a berry that is blue	*firefly* ≠ a fly made of fire	*bookworm* ≠ a worm in a book
	firefly = a fly that emits flashes of light like fire	*bookworm* = a person who loves to read all the time

Decodable Parts

Before asking students to decode compounds, be sure to choose words that contain letter patterns they have been taught. I often see lessons in which students are being asked to read a part of the word that is decodable, but the other part isn't. For example, *fishhook*. If students know short vowels and the *sh* digraph, then *fish* is decodable, but if they do not know the *oo* pattern, *hook* will be a challenge.

Of course, no one has time to stay up all night grouping compound words by patterns! That's why Appendix A has a list of compounds by spelling pattern (e.g., CVC compounds: *bedbug, bedroll, sunlit, uphill,* Vowel Team Compounds: *daylight, footprint*). I suggest using these lists once students have mastered a pattern

Check Out My Handy Word List!

Do not try to come up with lists of compounds on your own because it is time-consuming. See Appendix A: Decodable Compound Words Grouped by Pattern.

in single-syllable words. For example, once students can fluently blend words with short vowels and digraphs and blends (e.g., *back*, *bend*, *drop*), they are ready for a compound such as *backdrop*. You do not have to wait until students have mastered all vowel patterns before you start teaching compound words.

Cut-Apart Compounds

As with many big words, compound words can be cut into parts and reassembled. Start with words that share the same first part, such as *rainbow*, *raindrop*, and *raincoat*. This consistency helps students to see the two words. They can look down the row and see the word *rain* in each compound and then segment it from the second word. From there, move to compounds with different first words. This requires more analysis on the part of the student to find the words in the compound.

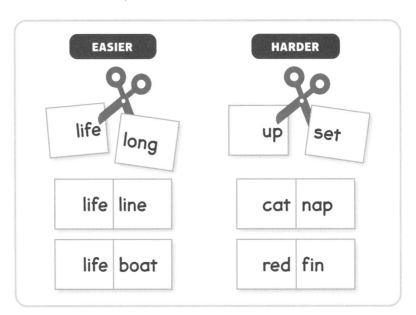

Compound Sorts

Choose two sets of words, each containing the same word part in either the beginning or end position of a compound, such as *back* and *bed* (see the chart on the following page). Scramble the words and then have students read each compound and place it in the appropriate column (e.g., "back" words, "bed" words). After sorting the first time, have students

Watch "Compound Sorts."

re-sort the words by those that have the target part at the beginning (e.g., *bedroom*) and those that have it at the end (e.g., *hotbed*). Working with compounds containing shared words in both positions builds flexibility.

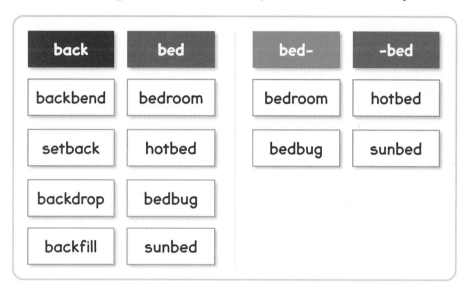

Build It

Identify a list of compound words that share at least one word (e.g., *fishbowl, sunfish, catfish, fishnet, starfish*). Write the shared word on an index card and write the other words on their own cards. Place the shared word on the left side of the desk and the other words on the right. Have students read all the words. Dictate the two words that form the compound and have the students create the compound with the cards. For example, "Please pull *fish* and *star* and make a compound. Remember, the shared word, *fish*, can be at the beginning or the end." You can also play by having students read all the word parts, combine them into compounds, and then share those with a partner.

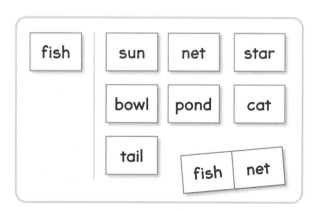

How to Teach It: Contractions

The activities that follow show students how to build contractions (e.g., *I have* > *I've*) and then match contractions with the two words they represent (e.g., *can't = cannot*).

Contraction Machine

There are many forms of this game out there. The idea is that two words go into the "machine," a rule is applied, and a contraction pops out. "Contraction Machine" is a good activity when students are first learning a certain group of contractions (e.g., contractions with the word *not*—*can't*, *don't*, *isn't*). It gives them practice applying the rule repeatedly.

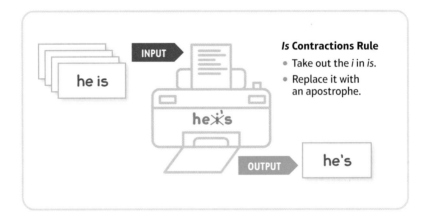

Missing Letter

For this game, students must read contractions and identify the letters that the apostrophe has replaced, as well as the two words that make up the contraction. Using a chart like the one below, they use a caret to "add in" the missing letters and then write both words.

	aren't	isn't	would've	I'd
Missing Letter	^o	^o	^ha	^woul
Two Words	are not	is not	would have	I would

Contraction Bingo

Once students have learned the basics of forming contractions, play "Contraction Bingo"! The version here shows contractions on the caller's cards and the two words of each of those contractions on the board. The caller draws a card, and says the contraction, and then the players mark the box with the two words on their board, if they have them. Of course, the game works the other way, with the board containing contractions and caller's cards containing the words in those contractions.

B	I	N	G	O
has not	they will	it is	they have	cannot
she is	have not	we would	we were	are not
they have	we will	is not	they are	he is

we'll   he's   it's

Match

This game gets students up and moving around. Create two sets of cards: one with contractions written on them and one with the two words that form those contractions. Distribute all cards to students and have them find the person with the card that matches their contraction or two words. I set a timer (one minute for 20 students) to keep students from standing around too long once they have found their match. Students love this game. It is a good time filler when you are waiting between subject blocks or right before lunch when everyone is antsy.

they've   they have   is not   isn't

How to Teach It: Inflections Without Spelling Changes

Inflections are typically introduced in kindergarten and first grade with base words that do not require spelling changes, and then the same inflections are revisited in second grade with base words that do require spelling changes (see Chapter 7). Most of the activities in this section can be used in all three grades, with a few exceptions, depending on the words you choose. The activities are presented from least to most challenging based on the demands of the tasks, described below:

1. **Least Challenging:** Add an inflection to a base without spelling changes (e.g., *get/gets, test/testing, bag/bags, fish/fishing*). Give students a single-syllable base word, have them add the inflection, and decode the new word. It starts with what students know, the base.

2. **Challenging:** Find the base in an inflected form of the word. Give students an inflected form of a word where the spelling of the base word has not changed (e.g., *trees, tested, fishing*). Ask students to identify the base word. This is more challenging because the student must do the work of finding the base.

3. **Most Challenging:** Apply a variety of inflections to one base word. Once students can add inflections to words and find them in words, they can review and practice different types of inflections across words. This can be challenging because some words require no spelling changes when adding -*s* but do when adding -*ing, -er, -ed* and vice versa.

Word Equations

With the word equations at this stage, students are only doing "addition," because there are no spelling changes and they don't have to take any letters out. Students start with a base word and then build that word up by adding inflectional suffixes. When the base word requires no spelling changes, the equations are only addition. Here's an example:

- *cats = cat + s*
- *cat + s = cats*

A good way to teach this is by creating equations with the blank spaces at different points in the equation. The easiest exercise requires students to combine the parts, without a spelling change: *cat + s = _____*. More challenging exercises contain blanks in other parts of the equation. As students work to figure out what part goes in the blank (e.g., base or suffix), they must analyze the fully inflected form—for example, "Okay, this says, *cats* = *cat* + _____. So, what is missing? Let me look at the word before the equal sign, *cats*. Oh, there is an *-s* on that word, *cats*. An *-s* goes into that blank." Once students have received sufficient practice on word equations you give them, have them come up with their own.

Draw an Inflection, Write the Words

This game can be played in small groups or pairs. Create cards with base words and cards with inflections and put them in two separate piles. Make sure students know how to add inflections to the base words you choose. Don't choose *baby*, for example, if you haven't taught change *y* to *i* + *es*. Have students draw a base word from one pile and an inflection from the other, and then have each student write the word on a dry-erase board. I like this game for three reasons: 1) *every student* is participating, 2) spelling practice cements the word knowledge, and 3) what students write is a great formative assessment. If you look at students' list before you review the correct answers with them, you can see what they know and don't know.

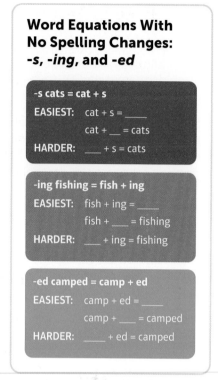

Word Equations With No Spelling Changes: -s, -ing, and -ed

-s cats = cat + s
EASIEST: cat + s = _____
          cat + ___ = cats
HARDER: ___ + s = cats

-ing fishing = fish + ing
EASIEST: fish + ing = _____
          fish + ___ = fishing
HARDER: ___ + ing = fishing

-ed camped = camp + ed
EASIEST: camp + ed = _____
          camp + ___ = camped
HARDER: ____ + ed = camped

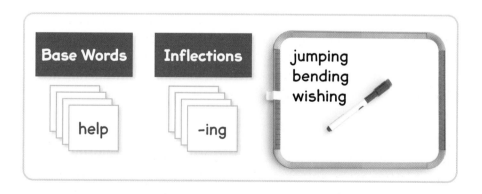

Base Words — help
Inflections — -ing
jumping
bending
wishing

Make It Big

Even in the early grades, children have the tools that they need to be able to take one base word and expand that word into five, six, or seven words by adding inflections or creating compound words. As phonics instruction moves into vowel patterns, and students begin mastering them, play "Make It Big." (See Appendix B: Lists for Make It Big.)

The first and most important step is choosing the base word because for this game, the base word should be one to which you can add inflections without changing the spelling. In this example, the word *cook* can easily lead to nine words without any spelling changes. Discovering and building multiple new words from a base word empowers students to feel grown up about big words.

Watch "Make It Big."

Preparation

1. Choose a base to which students can add endings (e.g., *-s*, *-ing*, *-ed*) and make compounds.

Have students:

1. Organize the cards as shown, in four columns.
2. Combine the base with each inflection and record the words (e.g., *cooks*, *cooking*) on a dry-erase board or in a notebook.
3. Combine the base with other base words at the beginning and end to make compound words (e.g., *cookbook*, *undercook*) and record these words as well.
4. Brainstorm and record other words that they can make with the base (e.g., *precook*). (This is a great way to see what they really know.)

2. Choose **inflections** that do *not* require a spelling change to the base.

3. Choose words that form compounds when attached to the base.

(before the base word)   (after the base word)

See Appendix B: Lists for Make It Big on page 148 for base words to use.

Find the Imposter

Watch "Find the Imposter."

To understand morphemes, students must know that every morpheme conveys some type of meaning. At times, sequences of letters that make up a morpheme are actually *not* a morpheme. For students to fully understand what a morpheme is, they must understand what it is not—a sequence of letters that *do not* carry meaning, per se.

For this variation on an activity designed for the upper-elementary grades by Goodwin et al. (2012), give students word lists with a particular letter sequence and have them identify which words contain the morpheme and which words don't. Below is a simple example with words that contain *-s*, which you might consider for mid-to-late kindergarten.

~~has~~   cats   ~~is~~   ~~kiss~~   dogs

And here are more advanced examples for *-ing* and *-ed*:

- sing   taking   singing   swing   ringer
- bed   netted   educates   tested   carried

Choose the Right Words

Most of the research-based activities in this section involve "word engineering" because they require students to break words into parts (e.g., *snow-ing, cat-walk, bab-ies*) or put parts together (e.g., *pat + ing = patting, hill+top =hilltop*). By doing that, students come to understand how the parts work.

A key ingredient to the success of these activities is choosing the right words. How many times have you been in the middle of a lesson and gotten off track because you were trying to come up with words on the fly? That has certainly happened to me. That doesn't need to happen. Just jot down the words you are going to use on a sticky note ahead of time.

In Closing, Remember...

Learning big words in the early grades requires courage on students' part, and teaching them requires it on your part! If you're like me, a longtime primary-grade person, it can be unsettling to dive into content that you are still learning yourself or that you are not used to teaching. The truth is, adding in big-words content does *not* change instruction that much. Phonics instruction in the primary grades should still focus mostly on single-syllable words, without excluding appropriate, accessible big words. Remember these points:

- Follow a scope and sequence that weaves in big-words instruction as you go.
- Before delving into compound words or inflections, make sure students can decode the patterns in the single-syllable words they contain (e.g., *cookout, cooked, outing*). A good rule of thumb: They must be able to read the single-syllable word to read a longer word.
- Don't lose sight of the importance of teaching the concepts around morphology. A big part of what we do in the primary grades is set the stage for learning in later grades, when big-words content really takes off. Also, students need to understand that words (free morphemes) are also *base words* to which other parts can be added (e.g., *prefixes, suffixes*).
- Keep active learning at the center of instruction. Learning words of any kind is like playing with LEGOs—kids manipulate words just as they manipulate LEGOs. They build words, take them apart, put them together, add letters, remove letters, and so forth. Because graphemes and phonemes are generally not meaning-based, we primary-school teachers are not used to asking students what word parts mean. But the entire point of morphology is to help students move toward full understanding of all the parts of the English language to become expert readers.

Syllables and Syllable Types in Grades 1-2

Anita, an experienced second-grade teacher in Arizona, explains, "I heard about syllable types and learned them in an in-service training, and it made sense to me. But I didn't really know what to do with the information. I taught the kids the name of each type and showed them a few sample words, but I didn't know exactly what else to do."

Anita is like many teachers right now, awash in labels and linguistic content, but uncertain about how to *use* that content. This chapter addresses how and when to teach syllables and syllable types to help students read multisyllabic words, and provides research-backed, engaging activities for doing so.

What to Teach: Syllables and Syllable Types

In this section, I give you just the "need-to-know" information for teaching syllables and how they work.

Syllables

A syllable is a unit of sound or pronunciation (e.g., *ap-ple*). It is the smallest unit that can be spoken with one push of breath and without distortion (Eldredge, 2005). Here are some other facts about syllables:

- Each syllable has at least one vowel sound. The vowel is the nucleus of the syllable. Some syllables also have consonants at the beginning or end (e.g., *stream*-er).
- Syllables *can* be units of meaning when they're entire words (e.g., *go*) or morphemes (e.g., *pre*-coat, rid-*ing*).
- But not all syllables are units of meaning/morphemes (e.g., *fan-tas-tic*)
- Phonics or phoneme-grapheme matching is the best way to teach for two reasons:
  1. The basic grapheme-phoneme pronunciations that young children learn work within a syllable (e.g., *cat, trip*).
  2. Vowel sounds often shift in pronunciation even if they share the same morphemic heritage (e.g., *electric/electricity*; *sign/signal*).

A good way to teach students to find syllables in words is by having them find the vowels first, keeping in mind that two or more adjacent letters may represent a vowel sound (e.g., *eigh, aw, oi, ay*). Researchers have found that teaching older struggling readers to break words orally by syllable and then to spell the syllables helps them to read complex words related to science and social studies (Bhattacharya & Ehri, 2004; Powell & Aram, 2008; Shefelbine, 1990).

Syllable Types

To help students read multisyllabic words, educators have organized syllables into six types based on vowel sound: closed, open, silent *e*, vowel team, *r*-controlled, and consonant -*le*. (In reality, these six types do not cover all the possible syllables, but they cover the most common ones.) See the chart on the following page for definitions and examples of each type. Syllable types help students read multisyllabic words by giving them patterns to look for. So, if students come to a word such as *perfect*, they can look for parts that they can read (e.g., *r*-controlled: *per*-, closed: *fect*).

English is not a syllabic language, meaning its smallest units are not syllables, but rather phonemes or speech sounds. If English were syllabic, we would use symbols for each *syllable*, not letter. As Moats and Brady (2000) state, "Our print systems do not represent separate syllables directly; they represent phonemes and morphemes. The syllable chunks that students can be taught to identify are the contrivance of scholars, a tool for attacking longer words."

Why Teach Syllable Types?

Syllable types are typically taught in first and second grades. The idea is to teach students to find syllable patterns in words. To me, syllable types are an intermediary step between the phonemic and more advanced morphemic layers of English. Syllable types work best in words that have a single, unbound morpheme as the root but with multiple syllables (e.g., *animal*). If a word has multiple morphemes in it (e.g., *predetermine, undoing, action, running*), I suggest having students find those morphemes to decode the word, because morphology is the basis of how English works, not syllabication. If a student can find a word's morphemes, then that's the way to go. If the word does not contain multiple morphemes, or contains morphemes the student does not know, then teaching syllable types is the way to go.

Type	Description	Sample Words	Notes
Closed	A syllable that is closed off at the end by one or more consonants. Vowel: short or lax	*cup, dig, button, match, rust*	The most common and consistent syllable type. This syllable type forms over 50 percent of all English syllables. Common in Anglo-Saxon words and Latin roots. Exceptions: -ld (e.g., *bold, cold*), -nd (e.g., *find, kind*), -olt (e.g., *colt, bolt*), -ost (e.g., *most, post*)
Open	A syllable that ends in a vowel. Vowel: long or tense	*go, hotel, be*	Very few single-syllable words in English have an open syllable (e.g., *me, be, she*). The open-syllable type is much more common in multisyllabic words (e.g., *ta-ble, ho-tel*). It is also common in Romance languages such as Spanish or Italian. Exceptions: *do, to*
Silent *e*	A syllable with a silent *e* at the end, signaling a long vowel sound. Vowel: long or tense	*place, theme, like, globe, mule*	This pattern is 75 percent consistent in single-syllable words, except for e_e words (Gates & Yale, 2011). Several o_e words are exceptions because they don't fit the pattern (e.g., *done, love, above, one, come, some, dove, glove, shove*).

Continued on next page

Type	Description	Sample Words	Notes
Vowel Team toast	A syllable that contains two or more adjacent vowels that represent one sound. Consonants may team with a vowel as well (e.g., *oy, ay, augh, ough, igh, aw*). Vowel: *lax* (short), *tense* (long), diphthong	*beat, greenhouse, play, toast, tool, boy, law, light, been, caught*	Many vowel teams come from Anglo-Saxon words whose pronunciations have changed across centuries.
r-controlled bar	A syllable that has one or more vowels + *r*. Vowel: *r*-controlled	*door, hairbrush, cart, burn, pair, deer, first, turn*	Sometimes this is called the "bossy *r*" because when the *r* is paired with a vowel, it kind of "takes over," and you hear the *r* more than the vowel sound.
Consonant -le (i.e., C-*le*) stable final syllable	A syllable that has a consonant + *le*.	*trickle, brittle, fizzle, pickle, tangle, castle*	Always in a word's final position. Some teach this syllable type along with -*el* words, such as *hotel, travel*. The second syllable has the /l/ sound and the *e* is silent. Only some consonants combine with -*le* (e.g., -*ble*, -*ckle*, -*cle*, -*dle*, -*fle*, -*gle*, -*kle*, -*ple*, -*stle*, -*tle*, -*zle*).
Leftovers odd and schwa	Syllables that don't fit any of the types above. Unaccented schwa spellings	*active, garage* *family, politics, company*	These patterns are not included in the syllable types.
Final stable syllable -tion, -sion		*action, vision, creations*	The -*tion* and -*sion* are not included in the six syllable types, but they are stable, final syllables.
Final stable syllable -ture		*puncture, capture, posture*	-*ture* is also a final stable syllable but is much less common than -*tion* or -*sion*.

There are several less common types of syllables that can still be used to help students decode multisyllabic words; for example, what some curricula call "stable syllables" (e.g., -sion, -tion, -ture) because they are highly predictable (e.g., confusion, transmission, action, section, picture, creature).

When to Teach It

Broad Scope and Sequence

As explained in Chapter 5, the very first multisyllabic words to teach students are decodable compounds (e.g., backpack, sunlit), contractions, and words with very common inflections (e.g., liking, waited). When do syllable types come into play? As this scope and sequence shows, right after those word parts. Most state and federal standards address syllable types in the first and second grade. Most teachers start teaching them in mid-first grade.

Broad Scope and Sequence

Latin and Greek Roots
Grades 4–5
▸ Derivational Suffixes
▸ Latin Roots
▸ Greek Roots

Prefixes and Suffixes
Grades 2–4
▸ Inflections With Spelling Changes
▸ Common Prefixes
▸ Derivational Suffixes

Syllable Types
Grades 1–2 *

Compounds, Contractions, and Inflections
Grades K–1
▸ Inflections Without Spelling Changes: Adding -s
▸ Inflections Without Spelling Changes: Adding -ing, -ed
▸ Compound Words
▸ Contractions

Adding Syllable Types to a Typical K–2 Phonics Curriculum

This chart shows you how to add instruction in syllable types to a typical K–2 phonics curriculum. The **green** rows contain patterns typically taught in K–2 phonics. The **blue** rows contain syllable-types add-ins, along with the add-ins from Chapter 5. For example, after teaching CVC words, add in labeling the closed and open syllable types.

Major Patterns Taught in K–2 Phonics	Example Words
Consonants and Short Vowels	
Short Vowel/CVC Words	hat, hit, net, top
Decodable compounds with CVC (Ch. 5)	catnap, bedbug
Inflections: add -s (no spelling change) (Ch. 5)	hats, hits, nets, tops
Syllable types: Closed (CVC), Open	go/got, no/not, so/sob
Contractions with 's	she's, he's, it's
Blends and Digraphs	trust, munch, test, fish
Inflections: -ed, -ing, -er (no spelling change) (Ch. 5)	trusted, munched, fishing
Decodable compounds with CCVC, CVCC, CVCCC	handbag, uplift, lunchbox
Syllable types: Closed (CVCC) or (CVCCC)	bent, trust, dish, munch
Contractions with 'll	he'll, they'll
Silent e	hike, tape, hope
Inflections: -s, -ing, -er, -ed (no change -s, drop -e) (Ch. 5)	hikes, hiked, hiking, nicer
Decodable compounds (Ch. 5)	baseline, icepick, timeline
Syllable type: Silent e	bat/bate, cap/cape
Vowel Teams	boat, seat, toil, shout
Inflections: -e, -er, -ed, -s (no spelling change) (Ch. 5)	boater, seated, toiling, greener
Syllable type: Vowel Teams	point, roast, peak
Contractions with n't	can't, isn't, wouldn't, couldn't
r-Controlled Vowels	bark, tore, first, term, turn
Inflections: -er, -er, -ed, -s (no spelling change) (Ch. 5)	barks, barked, barking, termed, harder
Syllable type: r-Controlled Vowel	hut/hurt, bark/back
Syllable type: C-le	trickle, puzzle, brittle
Review all syllable types and words with a mix of types	beetle, peacemaker, corner

Step 1: Label as You Go

Before students can read multisyllabic words, they must know how to decode common vowel patterns in English. After all, syllable types are based on vowels. So over the weeks and months that you are teaching vowel patterns as part of your phonics lessons, label the syllable types as you go. For example, *after* teaching short vowels in the CVC pattern, tell students:

> "This is called a closed syllable because the vowel is closed off by at least one consonant. In a closed syllable, the vowel is short. In the word *dig*, the last letter is a consonant. That *g* closes off the vowel, and the vowel spells the short *i* sound."

You could even have students code the vowel with a breve (ˇ). Not many single-syllable words contain open syllables, except for high-frequency words such as *no, go, so, be, we, she,* and *he*. So when you teach single-syllable high-frequency words, seize the opportunity to teach the concept of open syllables as well.

Label words with silent *e* and *r*-controlled syllables in the same way. When teaching silent-*e* words, contrast it with closed syllable words that can be converted to a silent-*e* word, for example *tap/tape, not/note, tub/tube*. When teaching *r*-controlled words, compare with close syllable words that can be converted to *r*-controlled with the addition of an *r*, such as *hut/hurt, cat/cart, shot/short*.

Labeling words containing vowel teams is a bit more challenging because there are so many of them. Vowel teams are typically graphemes made up of two vowels (e.g., *oi*, *ey*, *oo*, *ee*, *oa*) or a vowel and a consonant (e.g., *aw*, *ay*, *ou*). I use the term "vowel teams" instead of digraphs because some of the graphemes are made up of more than two letters, such as *igh* and *ough*. Words containing the consonant *-le* syllable are usually taught last because they typically contain more than one syllable.

I find teachers appreciate this streamlined approach, Label as You Go, for teaching syllable types. Valerie, a first-grade teacher in Cincinnati, explained, "I was intimidated by syllable types until I realized that I was teaching most of it already. I just needed to add the syllable type labels."

Step 2: Extend Study of Multisyllabic Words

The second step is to teach students to decode two- and three-syllable words by applying their knowledge of syllable types. This is much more intensive than Label as You Go, and usually takes six to seven weeks. Typically, teachers work on no more than two syllable types a week, doing the following:

- Reviewing the syllable type
- Comparing types through sorts or labeling
- Transforming one type to another (e.g., closed to silent *e*)
- Marking the syllable type in two- and three-syllable words (e.g., *bor-der*)
- Manipulating syllables to build words

After four to five weeks of learning all the syllable types, students spend the remaining weeks applying their knowledge to words that contain more than one type (e.g., *kindergarten*, *turtle*).

How to Teach It: Syllables and Syllable Types

The balance of this chapter is a collection of research-based activities for teaching syllables and syllable types. I begin with a process for teaching each of the syllable types (Knight-McKenna, 2008). (See Appendix C for a list of words organized by syllable type.)

Activities for Step 1: Label as You Go

Read Many Single-Syllable Words With the Syllable Type

During the typical phonics instruction, label syllable types as you go. For example, toward the end of teaching the vowel team syllable type, ask students to think of the many vowel teams they know (e.g., *ee, ea, oa, oy, oi, oo, ay, ai, aw*), perhaps showing them the graphemes on cards and asking them to name the sound(s) for each one. Then provide students with a collection of words and ask them to underline the words with the vowel team syllable type. Note this list includes words that have similar initial consonants but that *do not* contain the vowel teams (e.g., *tote/toast, peck/peak*) so that the students must really study the words.

tote	*toast*	*tap*	*boil*	*eight*	*egg*	*peck*
hot	*peak*	*see*	*bike*	*book*	*fray*	

Reviewing and reading the words together often leads to important clarifications for students. For example, sometimes vowel teams represent a sound that is neither long nor short (e.g., *boy, book, paw*).

Transform Single-Syllable Words

Transforming single-syllable words from one syllable type to another is a simple way to help students. The examples below show ways to transform open syllables to closed syllables, and closed syllables to silent *e*. This activity is best done using letter tiles for ease and efficiency. Have students say the words and note the changes in sounds.

Watch "Transform Single-Syllable Words."

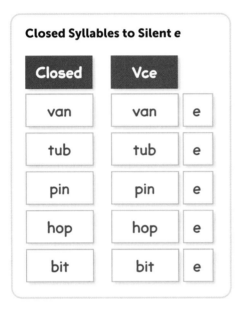

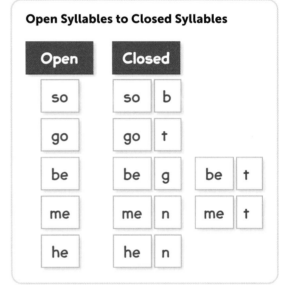

Sort Single-Syllable Words Into Syllable Types

Finding and comparing patterns is a process the brain does naturally. We clarify what something is by contrasting it with something that it is not. With that in mind, students can sort words according to the syllable types they've learned. The word *boat* is different from the word *bat* because two letters spell *boat's* long-*o* sound.

Closed	Silent *e*	Vowel Team
tap	bake	toast
peg	bike	boil
test		eight
		peak
		book

Rainbow Coding Words by Syllable Type

I am sure you have heard of Rainbow Writing words, where students write each letter of the alphabet in a different color. This practice has no research support because the coding is not based on graphemes (Jones et al., 2016). For example, each letter in a word such as *beat* would be in a different color, but the graphemes are actually *b-ea-t*. Color coding syllable types has not been specifically studied, but we do know that analyzing phoneme/grapheme relationships is phonics, which is a well-researched approach. Thus, students can identify syllable types by color coding them.

Word List		
1. hard	4. jerk	7. kite
2. trap	5. blow	8. pray
3. hive	6. go	9. part

Code
closed
open
vowel team
silent *e*
r-controlled

Activities for Step 2: Extend Study of Multisyllabic Words

Read the Syllable Type in Multisyllabic Words

After learning the syllable types in single-syllable words, students engage in an extended study of syllable types where they integrate their knowledge. This begins with reading multisyllabic words with the target syllable type.

Put together a list of words with a target syllable type in a multisyllabic word (see Appendix C: Two- and Three-Syllable Words by Syllable Type). Then ask them to read the words out loud and underline the syllable type in the word. You can see that this example focuses on vowel teams:

railr<u>oa</u>d   m<u>ai</u>ntain   rowb<u>oa</u>t

<u>oa</u>tmeal   r<u>ai</u>nb<u>ow</u>

Check Out My Handy Word List!

Do not try to come up with lists of two- and three-syllable words on your own because it can be very time-consuming. See Appendix C: Two- and Three-Syllable Words by Syllable Type.

Cut Apart Multisyllabic Words With Target Syllable Types

Students can also read and label lists of words or cut apart words containing the target syllable type, in this example, the silent *e* type. In the example below, each word has at least one syllable with the target type. The word *escape*, for example, has a closed syllable in the beginning but the last syllable is a silent *e*.

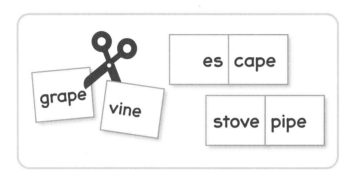

Search Texts for Words With the Syllable Type

Have students look for the target syllable types in books they are reading. Create anchor charts with lists of words that contain the target syllable type.

Sometimes students think they've found words that contain a target syllable type, but, in fact, they haven't. For example, students identified the word *around*, but the *ar* is not an *r*-controlled syllable type. I recommend discussing misidentified words with students along these lines:

> "I see this word *around* and it has *ar* but is that an *r*-controlled syllable type? Do we say ar-ound? No, the letter *a* in *around* is a syllable itself and it has the schwa sound like *uh*. That *a* does not go with the *r*. The *a* and the *r* are in different syllables, the *ar* in *around* cannot be an *r*-controlled syllable even though the two letters are next to each other."

If you are unsure about a word's syllable type, be honest about it. Tell students, "I don't know about this one, but I am going to look into it and get back to you." That way, you model inquisitiveness and a spirit of learning, which is just what learning about big words requires!

Sort Multisyllabic Words by Syllable Type

Sorting multisyllabic words by syllable type is an exciting and challenging activity. Most words have several different syllable types in them so students won't be able to sort those words into just one category. They must "dual sort" some words into two categories.

Watch "Sort Multisyllabic Words by Syllable Type."

Open	Closed	Silent *e*	*r*-Controlled	Vowel Team	Consonant-*le*
pi lot	nap kin	tooth paste	gar den	tool box	peb ble
ta ble	hic cup	in vite	her der	tooth paste	ta ble
	tool box				
	in vite				
	gar den				
	pi lot				
	peb ble				

For example, *toolbox* has a vowel team (*oo*) and a closed syllable. So students would place it in the vowel-team column with *oo* highlighted and also in the closed-syllable column with *box* highlighted.

Find the Vowels and Use Syllable Types

Because syllables are based on vowels, the most common strategy for helping students decode a multisyllabic word is to tell them to look for the vowel graphemes and then find syllable types. Many teachers ask students to mark the vowel(s) or vowel team(s) in a word by placing a dot under them. Then students identify the syllable types, decode the syllables, pronounce the word, and check to see if the word sounds like something that they know.

lo cal	*lo* = open syllable *cal* = closed syllable "*Local*? Yes. That's a word. It means near me."

The example below illustrates how a student might incorrectly group a vowel and consonant. By putting the *v* with the *o*, the student creates a closed syllable, *ov*, that does not sound like the beginning of the word *oval*. But when this student regroups the syllable to simply *o-val*, it forms a word.

ov/al	*ov* = closed syllable *al* = closed syllable "*Oval*? Not a word." Try again.
o/val	*o* = open syllable *val* = closed syllable "*Oval*? Yes. That's a word: the shape, an oblong circle."

Map, Code, or Scoop Syllables

Once students have learned the various syllable types, or have a strong handle on specific ones, they can map syllables on grid paper, code them with highlighters, or "scoop" them to identify syllables and group consonants with the correct vowels. For example, in a mapping activity, students can write each grapheme in a box, underline the vowel(s), and group the syllable(s) by "scooping" each one.

If two letters spell a single sound, or phoneme, both of them go in a single box. For example, the *or* in *corner* would go in a single box. For the silent *e*, the final *e* shares a box with the final consonant and is crossed out to show that it is silent.

A Commonsense Approach to Syllable Division

The chart below comes courtesy of Tory, a smart, helpful teacher I know, who said to me, "Look, I just tell kids what to look for—words, parts, prefixes, syllable types, anything you can see. Find it and use it." I like that idea!

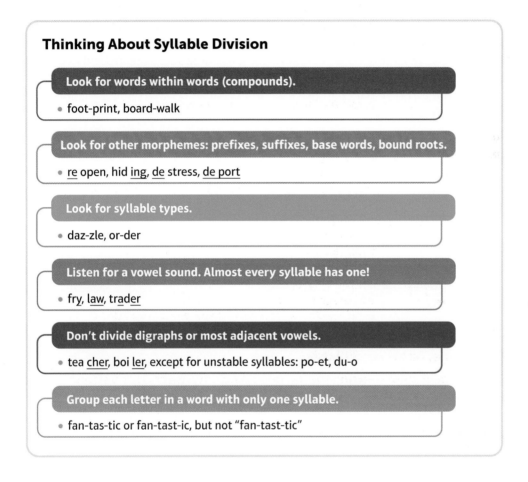

Thinking About Syllable Division

Look for words within words (compounds).
- foot-print, board-walk

Look for other morphemes: prefixes, suffixes, base words, bound roots.
- re open, hid ing, de stress, de port

Look for syllable types.
- daz-zle, or-der

Listen for a vowel sound. Almost every syllable has one!
- fry, law, trader

Don't divide digraphs or most adjacent vowels.
- tea cher, boi ler, except for unstable syllables: po-et, du-o

Group each letter in a word with only one syllable.
- fan-tas-tic or fan-tast-ic, but not "fan-tast-tic"

Shared Syllables

Some words share the same syllables. For example, *hamster* and *hammock* share the closed syllable *ham*. In this game, students look for the shared syllables in two or more different words. First, they read the shared syllable and then assemble that syllable (e.g., *per*) with a second syllable that forms a word (e.g., *fect, haps*). They must use trial and error to test if the shared syllable works with the other options. For example, "ham-haps? Not a word. ham-mock? Yes, hammock." Make sure that your students, especially multilingual learners, have the words they're building in their oral vocabularies. The activity can be done in two ways: 1) shared first syllables and 2) shared second syllables.

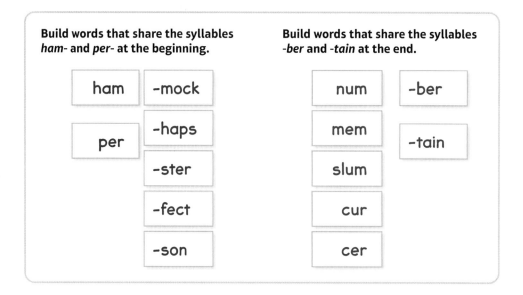

In Closing, Remember...

Teaching students about syllables and syllable types is an empowering way to introduce them to "big-kid words." Most educators use it in first and second grades as students are learning the many vowel patterns to show them how syllables come together in words (e.g., *button, castle*). There are a few things to keep in mind:

- Use syllable types to teach students to decode words with a single morpheme. Syllables are units of pronunciation, and each syllable must have a vowel sound. The six syllable types are: closed, open, silent-*e*, vowel team, *r*-controlled, and consonant -*le*. The syllable types work best for helping students decode words that have one unbound morpheme (e.g., *problem, fantastic*). When a word has more than one morpheme (e.g., *careful*), help them look for all of them, because these are the bases of the English writing system.

- Use a two-step approach for syllable types: Label as you go and extend study of multisyllabic words. As students learn to decode the vowel patterns in single-syllable words (e.g., vowel teams, silent *e*), label the syllable types, help students find the syllable type in single-syllable words, compare syllable types, and transform syllables. Once students learn all the syllable types, they are ready for a six- to seven-week unit in which they apply those syllable types in multisyllabic words.

- Keep students actively engaged in analyzing words and have them say the syllables and words as they do the activities. Have them find syllable types in words, assemble syllables into words, and break words apart by syllables. This provides practice in spotting syllables and becoming fluent with them.

- Remember that English is morphophonemic. As useful as they are, syllable types have limitations. English is morphophonemic, phoneme-grapheme units build morphemes. It is not a syllabic language, meaning that the visual symbols represent at the individual phoneme or speech sound level. For that reason, always encourage students to find the morphemes in words if they can. Morphemes help students to understand and decode words.

CHAPTER 7

Prefixes and Suffixes in Grades 2–4

I n a fourth-grade classroom I was visiting recently, the students got stuck on the word *interstate* during small-group reading. So the teacher started to unlock the word for them, using the six syllable types: open, closed, silent *e*, vowel teams, *r*-controlled, and consonant *-le*.

Okay, here is the word interstate. *Let's dot and underline vowels. Remember, more than one letter can show a vowel sound.*

I see four vowels and I think that some of them work together: Let's see, the I *in* in, *and then the first* e. *Does that* e *need to be grouped with a letter next door to it? Yes, it is* r-*controlled, so that should be* er *in* ter. *The* a *in* state. *How does that* a *work? Is it a short sound? No, it's a silent-*e *syllable type.*

So, the word is:

<u>i</u>n *(closed syllable)*   t<u>er</u> *(r-controlled)*   st<u>ate</u> *(silent e)*

"interstate" It's interstate. *What does that mean?*

This was good instruction. Fortunately, all the syllables in the word fit within the six types. But, I must admit, a different approach might've been more useful in fourth grade. In intermediate grades, word solving for typically developing students should bend toward finding morphemes, meaningful word parts, as opposed to syllable types. An intermediate reader in grades 3–5 would more likely analyze this word's base (*state*) and prefix (*inter-*). Even if the students were unfamiliar with the prefix *inter-*, analyzing this word's morphemes would have provided an opportunity to teach advanced reading, perhaps along these lines:

> *Okay, here is the word* interstate. *Now, we could dot and underline the vowels and look for syllable types, but I think you can handle something more challenging. Let's look for whole words, prefixes, and suffixes.*
>
> *Do you see a prefix, a suffix, or even a whole word?*
>
> *Yes, Ming found a whole word,* state. *Let me separate the word* state *since I know it and look at what's left.*
>
> > *inter   state*
>
> *Okay,* in *and* ter, *That is* inter.
>
> *Let me put inter with state,* interstate. *Do I know that word?* Interstate? *Oh yes, like the highway. An interstate. But what does that first part,* inter, *mean?*

If these intermediate students were struggling, I would have used syllable types. But they weren't, so I moved into structural analysis, or breaking words into meaningful parts.

As students move into the intermediate grades, we need to build their capacity for reading in middle and high school. In other words, our goal for them should not be completing elementary school, but rather being prepared for advanced, analytical, content-area reading in secondary school. Intermediate-grade readers must be able to decode and understand long words and, to do so, they must get to know affixes—prefixes, which change the meaning of words, and suffixes, which change the meaning and often their parts of speech.

There is a lot to do in the intermediate grades to get students ready for learning about prefixes and suffixes.

What to Teach: Prefixes and Suffixes

In Chapter 5, I discussed inflectional suffixes. Here, I go into greater depth about prefixes and suffixes.

Prefixes

The word *prefix* quite literally means "to fix before," and that is what prefixes do—they "fix" a morpheme at the beginning of a word to change its meaning, but not its tense or part of speech. They shift meaning in one of three ways:

1. To negate or deny the base word. For example, *nonstop* is quite dissimilar from its base word, *stop*.

2. To intensify the base word or make it "more than." For example, *overcook* means to do more cooking or to cook too much.

3. To change the base word's direction or position it in some way. So, *subgroup* means a group that is under or subordinate to a larger group, and *preorder* means an order that is placed before a product or service is available.

Three Ways a Prefix Can Change a Word's Meaning

– NEGATE
unlock, nonstop, misunderstand

+ INTENSIFY
hyperthermia, overeat, superhuman

↩ REDIRECT
preview, midway, review

For a complete list of prefixes, see Appendix D: Prefixes.

Many standards documents and curricula refer to teaching "common prefixes," and, of course, teachers want to know which ones are "common." The list on the following page contains 20 prefixes beginning with the most common (e.g., *un-*, *re-*) and moving towards those that are less common but still useful (e.g., *mid-*, *under-*). These 20 prefixes appear in 97 percent of prefixed words in books found in elementary classrooms (Carroll, Davies, & Richman, 1971). The first nine appeared in 75 percent of the prefixed words. You will notice that *in-/im-/il-* are listed twice. This is because those prefixes can have two different meanings. The most common is *not* (e.g., *illegal*, *impartial*) and the other meaning is *in* (e.g., *intake*, *implode*).

20 Most Frequent Prefixes in 97 Percent of Prefixed Words

9 Most Frequent Prefixes in 75 Percent of Prefixed Words			Next 11 Most Frequent Prefixes	
1. *un-*	not		**1.** *sub-*	under
2. *re-*	again		**2.** *pre-*	before
3. *in-, im-, ig-, il-, ir-*	not		**3.** *inter-*	between
4. *dis-, dif-, di-*	opposite		**4.** *fore-*	before
5. *en-, em-*	cause to be		**5.** *de-*	away from
6. *non-*	not		**6.** *trans-*	across
7. *in-, im-, il-*	in		**7.** *super-*	over, big
8. *over-*	over		**8.** *semi-*	half, past
9. *mis-*	wrong		**9.** *anti-*	against
			10. *mid-*	middle
			11. *under-*	under

(Carroll et al., 1971)

Most prefixes are only one syllable. In fact, the most common prefixes are an open or closed syllable type. Thus, prefixes are not hard to decode, and once students can identify the base word of a prefixed word, they will see its prefix. The trick is to help them detect when a group of letters is, in fact, a prefix and *adding meaning* to the word.

Most Words in Intermediate-Grade Texts Are Affixed in Some Way

Between 60 and 80 percent of the words that students encounter in grade 3 and higher have many morphemes, including prefixes and suffixes (Nagy & Anderson, 1984). Word-level instruction should not stop at upper elementary. It should shift to teaching prefixes, suffixes, and Latin and Greek roots systematically. The same amount of time that was devoted to phonics in primary grades should be devoted to word instruction in the intermediate grades.

To determine if a group of letters in a word *is* a prefix, students need to test it in two ways.

1. **Base word test.** Take the prefix or group of letters away. When you do this, are you left with a recognizable word? If so, the group of letters is a prefix (e.g., <u>un</u>tie = yes! <u>un</u>ite = no!) (Note. I talk about Latin/Greek roots in the next chapter so look there for an application of this test to bound roots.)

2. **Prefix test.** Take the group of letters and apply it to other base words. Do they form recognizable words with the same meaning at the beginning? (e.g., re > re<u>connect</u>, re<u>locate</u> = yes!; re > re<u>alize</u>, re<u>ckless</u> = no!)

Facts About Prefixes

- Added to the *beginning* of the word
- Change word meaning
- Are mostly bound and cannot stand alone
- A few prefixes are *also* words: *under, super, sub, over*

Suffixes

Suffixes are parts that are added to the ends of words and most often influence grammatical information. They often change the spelling and pronunciation of the base word, depending on how the base word ends. For that reason, suffixes can be challenging to students—more so than prefixes. When you add *-ness* to the word *happy*, you change the *-y* to *i* and then add *-ness*.

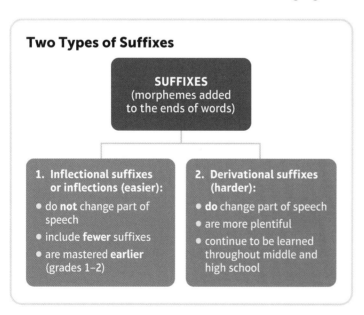

Two Types of Suffixes

SUFFIXES
(morphemes added to the ends of words)

1. **Inflectional suffixes or inflections (easier):**
   - do **not** change part of speech
   - include **fewer** suffixes
   - are mastered **earlier** (grades 1–2)

2. **Derivational suffixes (harder):**
   - **do** change part of speech
   - are more plentiful
   - continue to be learned throughout middle and high school

As I mentioned in Chapter 5, there are two different types of suffixes and this matters for teaching because one tends to be easier. The two types are: a) inflectional suffixes (also called inflections) and b) derivational suffixes. Inflections are usually easier and inflections without spelling changes are easiest (see Chapter 5). As students move into second grade, they learn how to add inflections when the spelling changes (e.g., *hit > hitting, baby > babies*), a content covered here in Chapter 7. Derivational suffixes begin in second grade and continue through the intermediate grades and then into high school and beyond (e.g., *-ify, -ic/ical*).

The chart below shows the 20 most frequently used suffixes in elementary school. The list has both inflections, marked by asterisks, and derivational suffixes. Notice *-er* is listed twice because, as detailed in Chapter 5, it has two meanings "one who" (e.g., *teacher, player*), which is a derivational suffix, and the comparative form, which is an inflection and also less common (e.g., *red, redder, reddest*).

> For a complete list of suffixes, see Appendix E: Suffixes (Inflectional and Derivational).

20 Most Frequent Suffixes

10 Most Frequent Suffixes	Next 10 Most Frequent Suffixes
1. *-s/-es**	1. *-ity, -ty*
2. *-ed**	2. *-ment*
3. *-ing**	3. *-ic, -ical*
4. *-ly*	4. *-ous, -eous*
5. *-er* (one who)	5. *-en*
6. *-ion, -tion, -ation, -ition*	6. *-er** (comparative)
7. *-able, -ible*	7. *-ive, -ative, -itive*
8. *-al, -ial*	8. *-ful*
9. *-y*	9. *-less*
10. *-ness*	10. *-est** (superlative)

*= inflectional suffix   (Carroll et al., 1971)

Inflectional Suffixes With Spelling Changes

Inflections are described in detail in Chapter 5. But here are a few reminders:

- *Inflect* means to change, alter, or modify.
- An inflection is a form of suffix.
- It is a morpheme added to a base word that may be a noun, verb, or adjective.
- It expresses grammatical information:

-s	animal*s* (more than one)
-ing	pitch*ing* (happening now)
-s	run*s* (third person singular)
-ed	help*ed* (happened in the past)
-est	happ*iest* (comparative-most)

- It modifies a word *without* changing its part of speech.

animal is still a noun when an *-s* is added
pitching is still a verb when *-ing* is added
happiest is still an adjective when *-est* is added

Adding *-s* and *-es*

When should you add *-s* vs. *-es*? I suggest following this handy little "rule" from Denise Eide (2012): If the sound at the end of the base word makes a "hissing" sound, as in *bus*, then add *-es*. The same holds true if the base word ends with /ch/, /sh/, /zh/, /j/, /x/, and /z/. Try saying *munchs*, *kisss*, or *fizzs*.

K–1: Just add *-s* to most words:

knobs, days, dads, bags, looks, teams, hops, totes, bars, boats, leaves, rows, toes, posts, jumps, holds, balls, crawls, boys, pokes

Late 1–2: If the word's ending "hisses" or "buzzes," add *-es*:

- /ch/ munches, touches
- /s/   kisses, blesses, passes
- /sh/ wishes, ashes, pushes
- /zh/ mirages
- /x/ coaxes
- /z/ fizzes

Note: Add *-s* after vowel teams that end in y (e.g., *-ay, -oy, -ey*).

(Eide, 2012)

You see? That /e/ before the -s at the end actually has a purpose: It allows you to *hear* the s!

Irregular Plurals

Irregular plurals are ones that fit into several categories. For many words that end in *fe* or *f*, you change the ending to *ves* (e.g., *loaves, wives*). In some words, the vowels shift when the word is plural (e.g., *man/men, goose/geese*) and in other words, the singular and plural forms are the same (e.g., *deer, sheep, teeth, fish*).

Changing *y* to *i*

What about words that end in -y? What do you do with those? Most teachers have heard the rule, "Change the *y* to *i* and add -es," but this rules does not apply in all situations. To decide if you should change the *y* to *i*, you must look at the letter that comes right before the *y*.

- Is there a consonant before the *y* (e.g., *try, baby*)? Change the final *y* to *i* and add -es, -ed, -er, or -est (e.g., *spies, babied, tried, happier, happiest*).
- Is there a vowel before the *y* (e.g., *play, annoy*)? Don't change the *y* to *i* just add -s, -ed, -ing, -er (e.g., *stayed, keys*).
- Do not change the *y* to *i* when adding -ing (e.g., *frying, babying*).

Adding -*ing*, -*er*, -*ed*

In Chapter 5, I introduced how to add -ing, -er, -ed when the base word's spelling does not change, as in *colder, fishing*, and *sleeping*. In early second grade, move to inflections that require spelling changes. In words with a silent *e*, the *e* is dropped before adding -ing, -er, or -ed (e.g., *noting, noted*).

Adding -*ing*, -*er*, -*ed*, Part I

Start Here, Early Grade 1:

No change

- If a word ends in two or more consonants (e.g., *dish, test, munch*)
- If a word ends in a vowel team and consonant (e.g., *heat, down, sight*)

boat > boating
fish > fisher
tow > towed
look > looker

Then Go Here, Late Grade 1:

Drop -e

- When a word ends in silent *e* (e.g., *like, take, hope, tube*), drop the *e* and add -ing, -er, or -ed.

like > liked
take > taker
hope > hoping
tube > tubing

When the base word is a CVC pattern, double the final consonant before adding -*ing*, -*er*, or -*ed* (e.g., *bagging*, *clipped*, *redder*).

Some call this the 1-1-1 rule. When a word is one syllable, with one vowel, and one consonant (CVC), double the final consonant before adding -*er*, -*ed*, or -*ing*.

When adding only -*er* or -*ed* to words ending in *y*, follow the "change the *y* to *i*" pattern. Remember that this pattern does not apply when adding -*ing* to a word ending in *y*.

Adding -*er*, -*ed*, -*ing*, Part 2

Start Here, Early Grade 2:

Double the Consonant

- When a word ends in one vowel and one consonant (e.g., *get*, *strap*, *shop*, *hit*: close syllable), double the final consonant and add -*ing*, -*er*, or -*ed*.

  get > getting
  strap > strapped, strapping
  shop > shopper, shopped, shopping
  hit > hitter, hitting

Then Go Here, Late Grade 2:

- Is there a consonant before the *y*? Then change the final *y* to *i* and add -*es*, -*ed*, -*er*, or -*est*.

  spy > spies, baby > babied, happy > happiest

- Is there a vowel before the -*y*? Then do not change the *y* to *i*.

  play > player, annoy > annoyed

- Do not change the *y* to *i* when adding -*ing*.

  fry > frying, buy > buying

Derivational Suffixes

Derivational suffixes usually shift the word from one part of speech to another. For example, *danger* (n) + -*ous* = *dangerous* (adj). The word *derivational* comes from the word *derive*, meaning to flow from or come from. And the word *derive* comes from the French word *deriver*, of the river, suggesting a seamless connection or extension to something. Thus, derivational suffixes transform a base word into many different words that are related in meaning.

Derivational suffixes allow us to expand base words horizontally, meaning we can change a word's purpose (noun, verb, adjective, adverb) without changing the idea it represents. The forms of *excite*, for example, represent different parts of speech, but they all relate to the idea of being enthusiastic or

Adjective- and Adverb-Creating Suffixes

Suffixes That Turn Words Into Adjectives

- **-able/-ible***: being able to (*visible*)
- **-al***: relating to (*musical*)
- **-en***: made of or full of (*wooden*)
- **-ful***: full of (*joyful*)
- **-ic/-ical***: characteristic of (*electrical*)
- **-ive***: tending to (*talkative*)
- **-less***: lack of (*careless*)
- **-ous***: full of (*glorious*)
- **-y***: state of (*grumpy, jumpy*)

Suffixes That Turn Words Into Adverbs

- **-ly***: how it is done (*quickly*)
- **-ward**: how it is done (*northward*)
- **-ways**: how it is done (*sideways*)
- **-wise**: how it is done (*stepwise*)

*in the 20 most frequent suffixes

energized about something. Students need to understand that concept—to understand the *why* of derivational suffixes and understand what those suffixes do.

Derivational suffixes are often layered on top of inflectional suffixes. For example, the word *excitedly* contains both the inflectional past-tense marker *-ed* as well as the derivational adverb marker *-ly*. A derivational suffix comes after an inflectional suffix. Derivational suffixes can be classified by the part of speech they form. On this page and the following page are lists of adjective-, adverb-, noun-, and verb-making suffixes, with the most common suffixes denoted by asterisks. As you can see, most form adjectives (e.g., *musical*, *glorious*). Adverbs are usually formed with an *-ly*, with a handful formed in other ways (e.g., *-ways, sideways*). Noun-creating suffixes, such as *-ion/-tion*, *-ment*, *-ity/-ty*, *-er/-or*, are quite common, whereas verb-creating suffixes are less common.

Derivational Suffixes That Do Not Change a Word's Part of Speech

-hood	state of being	boy = noun, boyhood = noun
-ism	belief or doctrine	patriot = noun, patriotism = noun
-ist	one who	chemistry = noun, chemist = noun

A few derivational suffixes are called "class maintaining" because they do not change a word's part of speech (e.g., *hood, neighborhood*).

Noun- and Verb-Creating Suffixes

Suffixes That Turn Words Into Nouns
- *-tion/-ion**: act or process of (*vision*)
- *-ment**: condition of (*excitement*)
- *-ity*, *-ty**: quality of (*equity*)
- *-al, -ial*: act or process of (*refusal*)
- *-er, -or**: one who (*visitor*)
- *-acy*: state or quality of (*privacy*)
- *-ance/-ence*: state or quality of (*entrance*)
- *-ness**: state of being (*happiness*)

Suffixes That Turn Words Into Verbs
- *-en**: become (*strengthen, tighten*)
- *-ate*: become (*differentiate*)
- *-ify, -fy*: make or become (*beautify*)
- *-ize, -ise*: become (*realize*)

* in the 20 most frequent suffixes

-en has two purposes:

1. **Adjective or Noun to Verb:** *-en* = become (*lighten*). This use is most common.

2. **Noun to Adjective:** *-en* = made of or full of (*golden*).

Facts About Derivational Suffixes

- A specific type of suffix that usually changes the part of speech
- "derive" means to come from, to descend from, to flow from, or be originated from
- Added to the end of a noun, verb, or adjective (e.g., *excitement, visible*)
- Modifies a word, usually changing its part of speech
- Expresses grammatical information

-ly	happy > happily (adverb)
-y	sleep > sleepy (adjective)
-ity	equal > equity (noun) or equality (noun)
-ical	music > musical (adjective)
-ness	sad > sadness (noun)

In elementary school, I recommend teaching the most common derivational suffixes—the ones that come up frequently in science, social studies, and math texts and discussions. There are so many derivational suffixes that it's a good idea to continue teaching them into high school and even college, based on the discipline.

Students encounter more derivational suffixes in advanced content-area texts because authors of those texts can encapsulate a great deal of information in a single word. For example, instead of writing, "Then the base chemical was enriched with oxygen," an author can write, "The base chemical was *oxygenated*." Converting a verb or adjective into a noun is called "nominalization," and it is common in the sciences.

What Makes Derivational Suffixes Challenging

Derivational suffixes can be challenging for students for these reasons:

1. **There are more of them than inflectional suffixes.** Inflections are a much smaller group of suffixes that are more constrained, meaning that content is specified, and you can teach it and be done. For example, it is not typical in seventh grade to teach adding *-s* or "change the *y* to *i* and add *-es*." Students are taught that, learn it, and know it. Derivational suffixes, however, are not as bound. Students will continue to encounter them as they move up the grades. Learning about derivational suffixes should continue into secondary grades and college (e.g., *-phillic, -phobic, -septic*).

2. **Unlike prefixes and inflections, derivational suffixes change a word's parts of speech.** Derivational suffixes are transformative—they change the purpose of words. This is the concept that we must build, and it is new and complex for many intermediate students. The idea of a word can be expressed as a noun, verb, adjective, or adverb by using a suffix.

3. **Derivational suffixes layer on top of base words, Latin and Greek roots, and inflections.** "Yeah, this is a complicated thing!" Stella, a fourth-grade teacher, said to me one day. I sympathize with her; derivational suffixes are the last layer of complexity that we add to words. I like to remind intermediate teachers that they are starting the deal with derivational morphemes, not closing it.

When to Teach It

Recently, I was working with Donna, a third-grade teacher, who disclosed, "I am a great reader and speller, and I understand a lot intuitively, but I don't know how to break down reading and spelling or explain them to kids." Boy, I shared that feeling as a young teacher! But as I started learning more, I became comfortable about what to teach when. You must use a scope and sequence that moves from the least complex to most complex patterns and categories. As with phonics, there is not one research-based, definitive scope and sequence for prefixes and suffixes but there are general principles and developmental guidelines to help inform a scope and sequence.

Broad Scope and Sequence

Beginning in second grade and continuing through fourth grade, students learn prefixes, how to add inflections where there are spelling changes, and derivational suffixes. From my perspective, inflections with spelling changes should be taught right away in second grade, along with common prefixes. Work with derivational suffixes might begin in second grade, continue into fifth grade and on into the secondary grades. Additional prefixes can be added in grades 3 through 5.

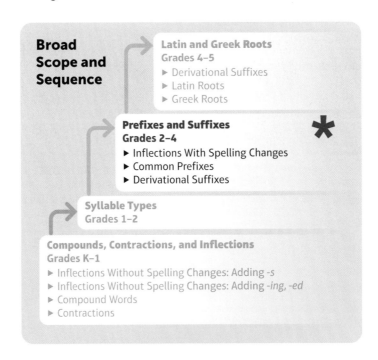

Broad Scope and Sequence

Latin and Greek Roots
Grades 4–5
▶ Derivational Suffixes
▶ Latin Roots
▶ Greek Roots

Prefixes and Suffixes
Grades 2–4
▶ Inflections With Spelling Changes
▶ Common Prefixes
▶ Derivational Suffixes

Syllable Types
Grades 1–2

Compounds, Contractions, and Inflections
Grades K–1
▶ Inflections Without Spelling Changes: Adding -s
▶ Inflections Without Spelling Changes: Adding -ing, -ed
▶ Compound Words
▶ Contractions

When You Teach a New Word, Teach Affixed Forms of That Word

The intermediate grades are where the rubber hits the road in big-words instruction. For every base word, there is a morphological family that can expand that word into as many as 10 additional words (e.g., *revolt, revolts, revolting, revolted, revolution, prerevolution, revolutionary, antirevolutionary*). The intermediate grades also involve a great deal of vocabulary learning. So, when you teach a word, also teach the expanded forms of that word.

Derivational Suffixes Should Be Taught Beyond Grade 5

Although few derivational suffixes appear in primary-grade texts, many begin appearing in texts for third grade and beyond.

In the primary grades, most students are not aware of derivational suffixes (Anglin et al., 1993). In third grade, they become aware of them as the language they hear and read becomes more sophisticated, and that awareness continues to grow in middle and high school (Carlisle, 2000). That means that we are *only getting started* teaching them in elementary school.

I would not avoid teaching simple derivational suffixes in the primary grades (e.g., *-ly, -er*) or even some challenging ones that intersect with science, math, or social studies (e.g., *-ology*). And I *would* avoid trying to cover them all in the intermediate grades.

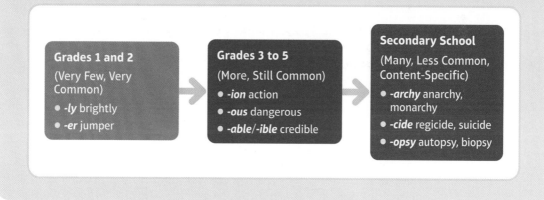

Grades 1 and 2
(Very Few, Very Common)
- *-ly* brightly
- *-er* jumper

Grades 3 to 5
(More, Still Common)
- *-ion* action
- *-ous* dangerous
- *-able/-ible* credible

Secondary School
(Many, Less Common, Content-Specific)
- *-archy* anarchy, monarchy
- *-cide* regicide, suicide
- *-opsy* autopsy, biopsy

Suggested Order: Prefixes and Suffixes

On pages 111 and 112, you'll find charts that suggest the order in which to teach prefixes and suffixes. Here are some guidelines for teaching:

1. Teach the Most Frequent Prefixes and Suffixes Early

Most standards documents will state that teachers should "teach common prefixes."

The first nine prefixes (e.g., *un-*, *re-*, *dis-*) and 10 suffixes (e.g., *-ly*, *-er/or*, *-ion*) listed in the charts on pages 111 and 112 appear in over 70 percent of affixed words (Eide, 2012). So it makes sense to teach those prefixes and suffixes first. (See Appendices D and E for complete lists of prefixes and suffixes.)

2. Group by Meaning or Grammatical Purpose Where Possible

Many scope-and-sequence documents group the most frequent affixes by meaning. For example, they group *number* prefixes (e.g., *bi-*, *uni-*, *tri-*) or prefixes that mean *not* (e.g., *-in*, *dis-*, *un-*) (Manyak et al., 2018). Derivational morphemes are often grouped by their function: noun-making (e.g., *-tion*, *-ment*), verb-making (e.g., *-ize*, *-ify*), adjective-making (e.g., *-ous*, *-al/il*, *-y*), or adverb-making (e.g.,*-ly*).

3. Pay Attention to the Transparency of Prefixes and Suffixes

The meaning of a transparent affix is recognizable (e.g., *non* means not, *ful-* means full of, *-less* means not a lot of). As such, students don't have to stop and think about them. They don't have to ask, "What does *-less* mean again?" They know it. The affix is easy to understand and remember. You might cover transparent affixes at the beginning of a unit because you can introduce the *concept* of affixes, without adding the burden of hard-to-remember meanings (e.g., *-ment*). For example, you might cover the suffix *-less* first because students can work on understanding that a derivational suffix changes the part of speech (noun to adjective/*time- timeless*), while not needing to learn what *-less* means.

The Most Frequent Prefixes

For the "Suggested Order: Prefixes" chart, I reordered the 20 most frequent suffixes listed on page 99. The reorganization considers meaning and transparency along with frequency. For example, in the following table, the first five prefixes listed are not the most frequent but prefixes among the top 20 that mean "not" (e.g., *un-*, *dis-*, *non-*). The prefixes -*in/im-/il-* are pushed down the list a bit because they are more difficult since they are "assimilated" prefixes and can be difficult to identify as prefixes (e.g., *invisible, illegal, illegible*). Position prefixes such as *sub-*, -*over*, and *mid-* are grouped together. This list is a good place to start, but in fourth and fifth grades, add less common prefixes, which you'll find in Appendix D.

Suggested Order: Prefixes

Prefixes	Example Words	Notes
un- (not)	unwrap, unleash, unbroken	
dis- (not, opposite of)	dishonest, disjoin, distrust	
non- (not)	nonslip, nonstop, noneffective	
mis- (wrongly)	mistake, misconnect, misread	
de- (opposite of)	defrost, deform, detrain	
re- (again)	retie, resell, recook	
pre- (before)	premix, pretrial, pretreat	
anti- (against)	anticrime, antibacterial	
in-, il-, im- (not)	illegal, immobile, inaction	Absorbed or assimilated prefixes that can be hard to spot in words.
en-, em- (cause to)	embark, enrage, encircle	
over- (over)	overeat, override, overrate	
sub- (below)	submarine, subdivide, subclass	
mid- (middle)	midnight, midyear, midweek	
under- (under)	undercover, underway, underwear	
super- (above)	superman, supersize, superheat	
in-, im- (into, in)	intake, inhale, imperil	Another less common prefix *in-/im-* meaning *into* or *in*
inter- (between, among)	interconnect, intersect	
fore- (before)	foretell, forehead, forewarn	
trans- (across)	transport, transmit	
semi- (half)	semicircle, semifinal	

Notice *in-*, *im-* are listed twice because there are two meanings for that pair. The more common meaning of that prefix is *not* (e.g., *invisible, illegible, immovable*), but it also means *in* or *into* (e.g., *imprison*).

Suggested Order: Suffixes

	Suffix		Example Words	Notes
	Inflections With Spelling Changes			
1	Add -es if the word "hisses" or "buzzes"		bunches, dresses, foxes, mashes	
2	Change y to i + es		fries, tries, babies, candies	
3	Change y to i + ed		cried, babied, supplied, partied	
4	Double consonant + -ed, -er, -ing		hopping, rigging, stopping	
5	Drop e + -ed, -er, -ing (review)		coping, baker, raked	
6	Change f to ves		wives, strives, loaves	
7	Other irregular plurals		fish, deer, man/men	
8	Comparative and Superlative -er/-est		red, redder, reddest	
	Derivational Suffixes			
1	-ly (characteristic of)	adjective > adverb	quickly, happily, kindly, likely, widely	Follow change y to i rule. Do not drop e.
2	-er/or (person who)	verb > noun	actor, governor, helper, swimmer	
3	-ion/-sion/-tion (act of, process)	verb > noun	subtraction, possession, creation	
4	-ment (action or process)	verb > noun	excitement, astonishment, merriment, pavement	Follow change y to i rule. Do not drop e.
5	-y (characterized by)	noun > adjective	glassy, glittery, itchy, whiny, sunny	Follow doubling rule. Follow drop e rule.
6	-ness (state of/condition)	adjective > noun	happiness, gladness, priceless	Follow change y to i rule. Do not drop e.
7	-ful (full of)	noun > adjective	plentiful, flavorful, cheerful, useful	
8	-less (without)	noun > adjective	penniless, spotless, toothless, clueless	
9	-ity/-ty (state of/quality of)	adjective > noun	loyalty, unity, charity, certainty	
10	-al/-ial (characteristics of)	noun, verb > adjective	comical, original, approval, colonial	
11	-ic/-ical (having characteristic of)	noun, verb > adjective	artistic, specific, historic, historical	
12	-en (full of)	noun > adjective	wooden, golden, ashen	Follow drop e rule.
13	-ous/-eous/-ious (full of)	noun > adjective	glorious, numerous, curious, courageous	
14	-ive/-ative/-itive (tending to, doing)	noun, verb > adjective	competitive, festive, cooperative, secretive	
15	-able/-ible (can be done)	verb > adjective	bendable, flexible, washable	Add -ible to a Greek or Latin root.

See additional derivational suffixes in Appendix E.

The Most Frequent Suffixes

The "20 Most Frequent Suffixes" chart on page 101 includes inflections and derivational suffixes. For the suggested order on the previous page, I grouped inflectional suffixes and then derivational suffixes. Because most inflections are common, I've listed them first and grouped them by spelling changes. I organized derivational suffixes by frequency but also addressed transparency (e.g., *ful-*, *less-*).

How to Teach It: Prefixes and Suffixes

A Routine for Teaching Prefixes and Suffixes

Strong word instruction of any kind is always explicit and systematic. That means it follows a scope and sequence, and the language we use is direct and clear.

Mesmer's Four-Step Compounds Routine

To introduce a new prefix or suffix, follow these steps:

1 Name the affix (e.g., prefix or suffix).

2 Pronounce it.

3 Define it.

4 Give an example of a word that contains the affix to illustrate its meaning. When choosing a word, make sure students know it and can read it. By doing that, you help them remember how the prefix or suffix works.

PQRST

PQRST was developed by Baumann and colleagues (2003). Working from left to right, students analyze words first for prefixes and think about their meanings. Then they look for the "Queen Root": the base word or Latin/Greek root, which carries the word's main meaning. Naming the root word "queen" serves as a great mnemonic because a queen is the most important person in a kingdom, just as the base word or Latin/Greek root is the most important part of an affixed word.

---

uncheerfully

1. **P**refix: *un-* (not)
2. **Q**ueen **R**oot: *cheer* (happy)
3. **S**uffixes:
   -ful (full of)
   -ly (doing something)
4. **T**ogether: doing without cheer

(Baumann et al., 2003)

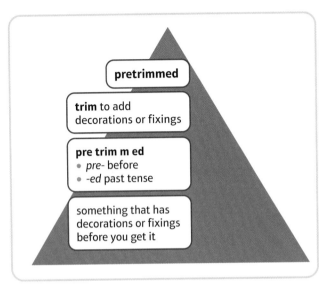

From there, have students look for suffixes and think about their meanings. Then have them put all the parts together and describe the entire word's meaning.

Another approach is to have students find the base word first and *then* examine prefixes and suffixes (Manyak et al., 2018). In a word such as *pretrimmed*, students look for the base, *trim*. In this word, the *-m* in *trim* has been doubled, providing an opportunity to remind students how sometimes we need to change a word's spelling when we add a suffix.

Quick-Read Affixes

Sometimes I see intermediate grade teachers drilling kids on "sight" words, and think, "What a waste of time!" For *most* intermediate-grade students, this is not appropriate because they already have many of those words in their vocabularies and are working toward reading them fluently in continuous text. What intermediate students need is to practice reading words that contain high-frequency affixes, a common recommendation in the research (Lovett et al., 2000; Toste et al., 2019). Simply create cards containing prefixes and suffixes you've taught and ask students to decode them, read them aloud, and state their meanings. Make sure they pronounce the affixes correctly. For example, the suffix *-able* is typically pronounced with a schwa sound *-uhble*, not with a long *a*, as in the word *able*.

Watch "Quick-Read Affixes."

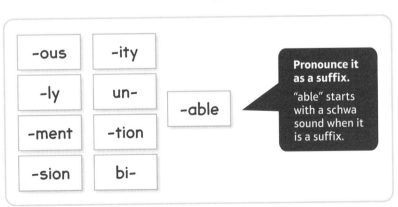

Hidden Word

Once students know a number of affixes, try this activity. Start by preparing a list of three-morpheme words that contain prefixes, base words, and inflectional or derivational suffixes (e.g., *misunderstanding*). Then create a card holder with three flaps to cover each part of the word.

Watch "Hidden Word."

To do the activity, give students small dry-erase boards. Flip up the first flap, name the prefix and its meaning, and have students write down all the words they can think of with that prefix. You might want to time this part to keep the pace brisk. Then flip up the second flap, read the base word, and ask students to combine base word and prefix and

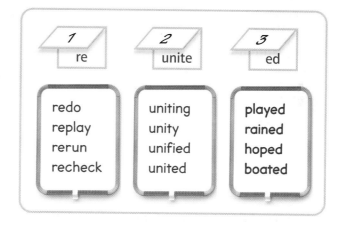

discuss what it means (how the prefix changes the base). Then have students write as many words as possible with the base. Before flipping up the third flap, ask students to hypothesize what the word is and then have students write as many words as they can with the suffix under the third flap.

How to Teach It: Prefixes

Build It

The "Build It" activity gives students practice in making prefixed words that are likely to be new to them. For the basic version, give students one prefix and a list of base words. Call out prefixed words and have students build the words with cards, spell them on dry-erase boards, or even write them on paper, so you can later assess. At the end of the activity, have students use the prefix to write other words that start with it.

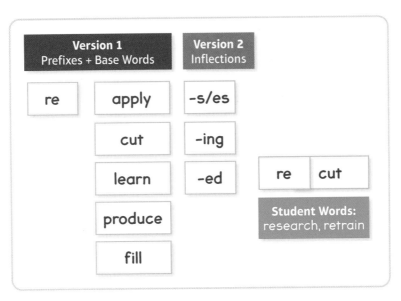

Version 1 Prefixes + Base Words		Version 2 Inflections
re	apply	–s/es
	cut	–ing
	learn	–ed
	produce	
	fill	

re	cut

Student Words:
research, retrain

For the more advanced version, have students also add inflectional suffixes to the prefixed words they build to layer in practice with inflections and their various spelling changes. Students will need to use dry-erase boards because of those spelling changes.

Prefix or Pretender?

We can learn what something is by learning what it is not. Often, students encounter a sequence of letters that makes up a prefix, but is *not* a prefix (e.g., *un-cle*). This activity helps them understand that prefixes add meaning to words. It also reinforces the fact that prefixes not only have grapheme-phoneme relationships, but also add meaning. Give students word pairs that begin with the same letters, some of which are prefixes and some of which are not (e.g., *uncle* vs. *unfold*) Then have them look at each word and determine whether it contains a prefix or not. If they can't explain how the unit adds meaning, it is not a prefix.

Watch
"Prefix or Pretender?"

unlikely	uncle
rebuild	realize
unfold	under
illusion	illogical
reunite	restful

(Blevins, 2023)

Prefix Sort

When students sort words by prefixes, they must analyze them and look carefully for meaning. Not every prefixed word will be clear to them. For example, they may not know the word *declaw* or *detrain*. Be sure to include a few pretenders, words containing the same letter sequence as the featured prefixes in the set, but without the meaning (e.g., *redcoat, dentist*). This encourages students to analyze the words, instead of visually sorting on autopilot.

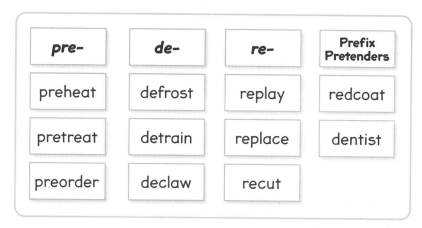

Anchor Charts

Anchor charts are great for collecting words, but it's important to use them for teaching, particularly teaching concepts that students may have difficulty grasping. In the example shown on the right, the meaning of the word *discover* was not clear to students, and, for that reason, the teacher put a question mark next to it. Working from the chart, she explained to students that *dis* means *not*, so to discover means to uncover or reveal. Also, the word *uniform* was mistakenly listed under the prefix *un-*. Students knew that *uniform* had a prefix, but they did not read far enough in the word to find the prefix *uni-*. So the teacher used that as an instructional point as well.

dis-	-in/-im/-il	un-
disrespect	immobile	unpopular
disorganized	illogical	unpack
discover?	inappropriate	undo
		uncheck
		unusual
		~~uniform~~

Notes:

dis-cover = not cover, to find out, to uncover

uni-form does not have the prefix *un-*, it has the prefix *uni-*, meaning one.
uniform = having one form.

How to Teach It: Inflectional Suffixes With Spelling Changes

Word Equations

When adding an inflection requires a spelling change, such as dropping the *e*, doubling the consonant, or changing *y* to *i*, the word equations will require addition and subtraction. Take, for example, adding *-ed* to the word *nod*. The equation requires adding both an extra *d* as well as the *-ed*. With the word *hoping*, subtraction comes into play because the equation requires the *e* to be dropped.

Word Equations With Spelling Changes: *-ed* and *-ing*

Doubling	Drop *e*
nodded = nod + d + ed	*hoping = hope - e + ing*
EASIEST: nod + d + ed = _____	EASIEST: hope – e + ing = _____
nod + __ + ed = nodded	hope – __ + ing = hoping
nod + d + __ = nodded	hope – e + __ = hoping
HARDER: ___ + d + ing = nodded	HARDER: _____ + e + ing = hoping

Word Equations With Spelling Changes: *-es* and *y* to *-i + es*

Add *es* if the word "buzzes"	Change *y* to *i* and add *es*
bunches = bunch + e + s	*fries = fry – y + es*
EASIEST: bunch + e + s = _____	EASIEST: fry - y + i + es = fries
bunch + __ + s = bunches	fry - __ + i + es = fries
bunch + e + __ = bunches	fry - y + __ + es = fries
HARDER: _____ + e + s = bunches	HARDER: _____ - y + i + es = fries

Find the Base, Code the Word

In this challenging activity, students start with a fully inflected word and move backwards to identify its base.

Give students a word with an inflection, such as *cries*, and have them write it at the top of a sheet of paper or dry-erase board. Then instruct them to break off the inflection (*-ing, -ed, -s/es)*. After that, they identify the base word. If the base was changed, they place a slash mark through letters added or add back a silent *e* with a caret (e.g., *hope*). Lastly, they write the correct form of the base word. As you can see, this is a complicated, multistep process that requires fluent command of the rules for adding inflections.

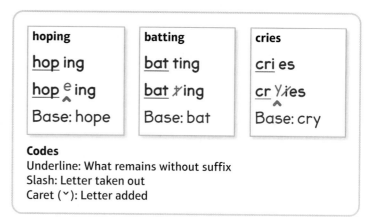

Codes
Underline: What remains without suffix
Slash: Letter taken out
Caret (˅): Letter added

The Three Sounds of *-ed*

The inflection *-ed* is a bit like *-s* in that students may see the letters *e* and *d* but hear one of three sounds.

When the base word ends in a sound that is unvoiced (e.g., /p/, /f/, /s/), the sound we hear is /t/ (e.g., *jumped, puffed*). When the base word ends in a sound that is voiced (e.g., /b/, /g/, /m/, /l/), we hear /d/ (e.g., *bagged, blamed*). When the base ends in /t/ or /d/, we hear /ed/ (e.g., *sprinted, binded*).

So, why does this matter when it comes to teaching kids how to read? We don't spell the past tense *-ed* exactly as it sounds, with a /t/ in *jumped* or the /d/ alone in *called*. That is not how morphemes work. I suggest showing students examples of the three different *sounds* that *-ed* can make:

- /d/: *filled, yelled, claimed, blamed, called, summed*
- /ed/: *listed, handed, melted, added, hinted*
- /t/: *puffed, backed, wished, kissed, fixed, lifted*

Irregular Plurals

Every letter pattern in the English language has exceptions, including plurals. Although we use -s to pluralize most words, we don't for all words. Give students a brief introduction to irregular plurals. Tell them some words require letter changes to show plurals (e.g., *loaf/loaves*), some words require vowel changes (e.g., *mouse/mice*), and others require no changes at all (e.g., *sheep, fish*).

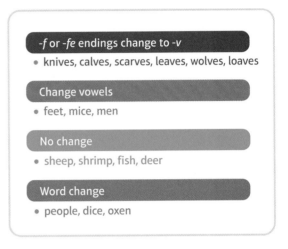

-f or -fe endings change to -v
- knives, calves, scarves, leaves, wolves, loaves

Change vowels
- feet, mice, men

No change
- sheep, shrimp, fish, deer

Word change
- people, dice, oxen

How to Teach It: Derivational Suffixes

Suffix Sort

Remember, derivational suffixes almost always shift a word's part of speech in some way. Students need to analyze suffixed words for their parts of speech. To prepare for this activity, create cards with words containing three different suffixes.

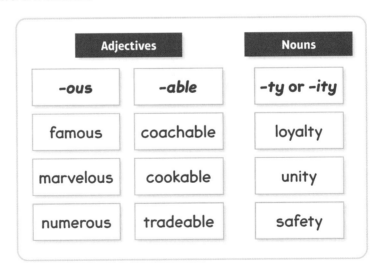

Adjectives		Nouns
-ous	**-able**	**-ty or -ity**
famous	coachable	loyalty
marvelous	cookable	unity
numerous	tradeable	safety

When a student is reading a book and comes to a suffixed word he or she doesn't know, the student can use what he or she knows about suffixes to discern information about the word. For example, if a student encountered *infection*, he or she would use both the context (e.g., a passage about polio disease) and his or her knowledge about the suffixes (e.g., *-ion*= noun-making suffix meaning "the process of") to figure out what the words means.

Word Equations

Give students a suffix bank and a base word bank and then have them create as many equations as they can. If you want students to focus on derivational suffixes, do not include inflectional suffixes (e.g., *-ed*) in the suffix bank. But once students are comfortable with derivational suffixes, including inflectional suffixes in the bank is a good idea. One caveat: Make sure that most of the suffixes can be added to more than one base word so that the activity requires students to do more than one-to-one matching of suffixes and base words.

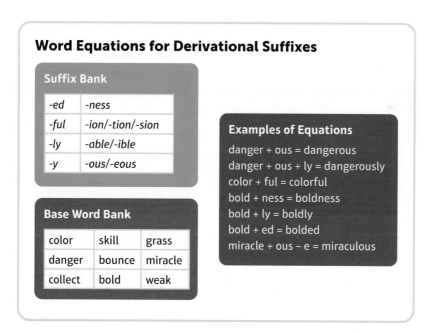

Word Equations for Derivational Suffixes

Suffix Bank

-ed	-ness
-ful	-ion/-tion/-sion
-ly	-able/-ible
-y	-ous/-eous

Base Word Bank

color	skill	grass
danger	bounce	miracle
collect	bold	weak

Examples of Equations

danger + ous = dangerous
danger + ous + ly = dangerously
color + ful = colorful
bold + ness = boldness
bold + ly = boldly
bold + ed = bolded
miracle + ous – e = miraculous

Fill in the Correct Word

As students work with derivational suffixes, they begin to understand that you can use the same idea but in different forms (e.g., noun-*courage*, adj-*courageous*, adv-*courageously*). This is the mark of an advanced reader and shows that students' morphological understandings are becoming nimble and flexible. In this activity, students choose the word with the appropriate suffix that matches a sentence context. What students enjoy most about this activity is that they get to choose suffixes to use in authentic writing. And, as a bonus, it's similar to what they're expected to do on many assessments. So it's a fun embedded form of practice.

Darron was a very fast runner on the team. He ran _____.

Out of all three runners Darron was the _____.

The coach told Darron, "You run with such _____."

Sheila challenged Darron to a race.
"I can run _____than you!"

Answer choices: *quick, quickly, quickness, quicker, quickest*

(Goodwin et al., 2020)

Give students several sentences with missing suffixed words, along with options for words to fill in. Their challenge is to not only select the right word (i.e., the word that makes sense), but also the one reflecting the right part of speech. Notice in the example that there are two potential options for the first sentence: *quick* and *quickly*. After filling in the blanks, discuss why each word fits a specific sentence by explaining the grammar: "Yes, for this sentence you need to use *quickest* because it is comparing three runners."

In Closing, Remember...

On the surface, prefixes and suffixes may seem straightforward, but they are not! There are several important points to remember:

- Prefixes, suffixes, and Latin and Greek roots are the second layer of decoding instruction. The field has simply not devoted enough attention to systematic, explicit instruction in upper-level word study. Yet, most of the words students encounter in grades 3 and above have multiple morphemes.

- There are two types of suffixes: inflectional and derivational. This matters for teaching. Inflections are taught and mastered earlier than derivational suffixes.

- Inflections do not change the part of speech of a word. They can be used to pluralize (e.g., *nuts*), mark verb tense (e.g., *tasted, tasting*), and signify comparisons (e.g., *pink, pinker, pinkest*). Introduce inflections in grades K–1 without spelling changes (see Chapter 5) and finish them up starting in grade 2 with words that involve spelling changes (e.g., doubling the consonant: *tapping*; changing the *y* to *i*: *happiest*).

- Derivational suffixes change the part of speech of most words. A word can become a noun, verb, adjective, or adverb, depending on the suffix (e.g., *polite, politeness, politely*). Many of them also require a spelling change to the base word. So just get started with derivational suffixes in elementary school because they will continue to emerge in high school and even college disciplines.

- Teach the most common prefixes and suffixes first. Most standards recommend teaching common prefixes and suffixes, but teachers often do not know what those are. In this chapter, I included lists of the 20 most frequent prefixes and suffixes. After teaching the most frequent affixes, see Appendices D and E for additional ones.

- Focus on meaning. As with all big words, make sure students understand the meanings of affixed words—and that includes the meanings of the affixes themselves.

CHAPTER 8

Latin and Greek Word Roots in Grades 4–5

Valerie, a veteran teacher of 20 years, loves teaching fifth grade, but noticed some gaps in her instruction:

I am a reading girl! I love teaching reading! My classroom is full of chapter books and fact books about science. I love working with kids in novel groups or unpacking a dense informational science text. We write stories, lab reports, historical fiction, field guides, and poems. And I have a strong vocabulary and comprehension strategy instruction program. But I realized that I was kind of throwing in word analysis here and there. Honestly, I found it boring and tedious.

After taking a class through my local university, my attitude changed. I could see that I was missing a big opportunity to set my students up for success—Latin and Greek roots! Until someone showed me all the different roots, I did not realize how powerful they really are. In fact, as I started to become aware of them, I saw them everywhere. Like the Latin root scrib/scribe and script. It's everywhere: prescribe, subscribe, scripture, inscribe, and describe. This year, I taught my students about 12 Latin roots and 12 Greek roots and it was so much fun! All year long, we were spotting these words, unpacking them, recording, and looking them up. We all became root investigators!

Believe it or not, I have heard so many teachers tell this story. Because they are so ubiquitous in English, teachers find that teaching Latin and Greek roots opens so many possibilities. As with all big-words content, however, you must understand it first. At the beginning of this chapter, I provide a quick overview of what bound roots are, and then give a little information about how Latin and Greek roots are different.

What to Teach: Latin and Greek Roots

Bound Roots

There are three types of bound morphemes, meaning units that cannot stand alone and must be attached to words: prefixes, suffixes, and bound roots, which include Latin and Greek roots. A *bound root* carries the main meaning in a word (e.g., *de-**scribe***) and must have some type of prefix or suffix added to it, to make it a freestanding morpheme or word (e.g., ***hydro**-plane*).

Base words are freestanding words or free morphemes to which prefixes and suffixes can be added. You can take off the prefixes and suffixes and still have a word.

Facts About Bound Roots

- Carry the main meaning in a word
- Are "bound," meaning they rarely can stand alone
- On occasion, may be freestanding words (e.g., *port, graph, photo*)
- Require prefixes and/or suffixes to become freestanding words: *aud-itory, tele-vis-ion*
- Are used in academic works, science, math, and social science

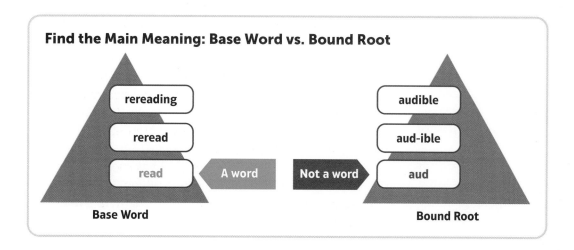

Find the Main Meaning: Base Word vs. Bound Root

rereading

reread

read

A word

Base Word

audible

aud-ible

aud

Not a word

Bound Root

For most students, bound roots are a new type of morpheme, usually the last type they learn. Teaching the concept can be tricky because students are used to roots being base words, or free morphemes, that can stand alone (e.g., **child**hood, re**test**ing). Because bound roots cannot stand alone and are not recognizable as whole words, students may have difficulty finding them in words (e.g., **vis**ion, **audi**ence). This is especially true if you do not teach the roots. Students must have exposure to Latin and Greek roots to be able to find them in words and decode those words. In comparison, because most students have been exposed to base words, they can usually find them by separating them from prefixes and/or suffixes.

Latin Roots

As I described in Chapter 2, Latin roots came into the English language around 1066 when Norman invaders came onto the British Isles, bringing with them words that were in their language from the Romans (Henry, 2010). These Latin words introduced more sophistication to the Anglo-Saxon base, which was used to describe everyday objects and actions. Latin became the language of the church and academy, which is why today's texts for secondary school and college contain so many words with Latin roots. Students cannot read anything beyond the easiest texts without running into a Latin root. The spellings of Latin roots most often follow simple spellings and usually do not have vowel teams (e.g., *cred, vis, struct, tract*).

Facts About Latin Roots

- Carry the main meaning in a word
- Are bound roots, meaning they cannot stand alone
- Require prefixes and suffixes to create words: *pre-scrip-tion, dis-rupt-ing*
- Are used in formal, academic, and literary texts

spect	*spectacular, inspection, respectfully*
tract	*detract, intractable, extract*
bio	*biosphere, biology, biochemical*

Greek Roots

Greek roots are similar to Latin roots, but there are some key differences to understand. Like Latin roots, Greek roots are bound, meaning they cannot stand alone as a meaningful word (e.g., *therm-, hydro-, auto-*). There are two main differences between Greek roots and Latin roots: 1) location of Greek roots in words, and 2) unique sound-spelling patterns.

1. **Location of Greek Roots:** Greek roots can be combined with other parts at the beginning or ending of words. For that reason, they are sometimes called "combining forms." For example, in the word *geography*, the Greek root *geo* (earth) is at the beginning, the root *graph* (write) is in the middle, and the suffix *y* is at the end. In contrast, Latin roots remain at the middle, with prefixes or suffixes added. For example, the Latin root *vis* appears only at the beginning or middle of the word, and never at the end, the way *graph* does (e.g., en-**vis**-ion, **vis**-ion-ary). Some Greek roots come at the end of words more frequently, such as *graph, gram, meter, ology, cracy, scope, polis*, and *crat* (Henry, 2010). Many more come at the beginning, such as *auto, phono, semi*, and *phys*.

2. **Unique Sound-Spelling Patterns.** Greek roots also have unique spellings with *ph* representing the /f/ sound, *ch* representing the /k/ sound, and *y* representing the short *i* sound. These spellings offer students a good clue that they may be working with a Greek root. For example, the *ch* in the root *arch* (definition: chief) actually has the /k/ sound in words such as *archaeology, architecture*, and *monarch*. Another example is the *y* in the root *syl* (definition: together with/jointly) found in the word *syllable*.

Unique Spellings in Greek Roots

ph = /f/	*phobia, photo, graph*
ch = /k/	*chronology, chorus, Christian*
y = /ĭ/	*physical, gym, rhythm*

Facts About Greek Roots

- Carry the main meaning in a word
- Are bound roots, meaning they usually cannot stand alone
- May have unique spellings (e.g., *ph* = /f/, *ch* = /k/, *y* = /ĭ/)
- Also called "combining forms" because they can be combined with other roots at any position in a word

  photographic, telephoto

  thermometer, geothermal

  dehydrate, hydrofoil, rehydration
- Are used in science and math

scope	*telescope, helioscope*
meter	*thermometer, speedometer*
bio	*biosphere, biology, biochemical*

Some roots have the same meanings and are spelled similarly. For example, you might find a word with either *duc* or *duct* to show the Latin root for "to lead" (e.g., *reduce, conduct, introduce*). Similarly, you might find a word with either *metr* or *meter* to show the Greek root for "to measure" (e.g., *symmetric, photometer*). I call these "siblings" because they are both from the same family and mean the same thing.

When to Teach It

Broad Scope and Sequence

Although instruction in Latin and Greek roots is the last topic I'm covering for K–5, your students will hopefully continue to learn about them into secondary school, college, and even their careers. That's how robust this topic is! Most teachers introduce students to the concept of "root" in fourth grade and cover the most common roots, and provide more focused instruction in fifth grade.

Broad Scope and Sequence

Latin and Greek Roots
Grades 4–5
▸ Derivational Suffixes
▸ Latin Roots
▸ Greek Roots

Prefixes and Suffixes
Grades 2–4
▸ Inflections With Spelling Changes
▸ Common Prefixes
▸ Derivational Suffixes

Syllable Types
Grades 1–2

Compounds, Contractions, and Inflections
Grades K–1
▸ Inflections Without Spelling Changes: Adding -s
▸ Inflections Without Spelling Changes: Adding -ing, -ed
▸ Compound Words
▸ Contractions

Suggested Order: Latin and Greek Roots

Although Latin and Greek roots function similarly and can be taught together, most curricula address them separately, at least at first.

Teach Latin Roots Before Greek Roots

Begin with the Latin roots because they do not have the combining features of the Greek roots, discussed in the previous section.

Start With the Most Common Latin Roots

As with other morphemes, start with the most common roots because students see them in many words when they read. The first chart below contains 10 common Latin roots, the ones to teach first, and the second chart contains Latin roots to move onto from there. I recommend identifying about two roots to teach each week and use activities to show how the roots can expand and form many words. Because words with Greek and Latin roots include prefixes, inflections, and derivational suffixes, when you teach them you're not only teaching roots, you are also revisiting a range of morphemes that students have learned to this point.

For a longer list of Latin roots, see Appendix F: Latin Roots.

Most Common Latin Roots

Root	Meaning	Sample Words
aud	to hear	audience, auditory, auditorium, audible
dict	to speak, say	dictate, predict, dictation, edict
ject	to throw	eject, reject, subject, project
port	to carry	transport, portable, report, porter
rupt	to break	erupt, rupture, disrupt, interrupt
scrib/script	to write	scribe, scripture, scribble, prescribe, describe
spect	to observe	inspect, spectate, spectacle, respect
struct	to build	construct, reconstruct, structure, instruct
tract	to pull	tractor, traction, detract, extract
vis	to see	visual, vision, supervise, visualize

(Blevins, 2023)

I once observed Shelley, a skilled fourth-grade teacher, lead a wonderful discussion about the word *conduct*. It went something like this: "I see this word *conduct*, but I am not sure what it has to do with the root *duct* and its meaning. I know that *conduct* has to do with electricity and wires, but what is

More Latin Roots

Root	Meaning	Sample Words
form	to shape	deform, uniform, reform
flect/flex	to bend	reflex, deflect, flexible
cred	to believe	credit, incredible, credible
duct/duce	to lead	reduce, produce, conduct
equa/equi	equal	equator, equinox, equity
grac/grat	thankful	grace, grateful, gratitude
sequ/sec	follow	sequel, sequential, sequence
vac	empty	vacation, vacate, vacuum
voc	call	vocal, vocation, invoke, revoke

(Blevins, 2023)

the leading part?" Because of the clues about electricity and wires that Shelley provided in her question, her students were able to come to the conclusion that *conduct* means leading through, as in leading electricity through the wire. After discussion, Shelley and her students looked the word up on etymonline. com, a website that provides the etymology and roots in words, and found that the prefix *con-* means "with." Thus, conduct means "with leading or guidance." The lesson for you here: It is not enough to just teach students roots and their meanings. We must unpack roots and other word parts to understand them within the context of words.

For a longer list of Greek roots, see Appendix G: Greek Roots.

Move On to the Most Common Greek Roots

Teach Greek roots after introducing Latin roots, starting with the most common ones. The first chart on the next page contains the 10 most common Greek roots, and the second chart contains roots to teach from there. As mentioned, Greek roots can occur at the beginning, middle, or end of a word. Start with roots that occur at the beginning of words because they are most similar to Latin (e.g., *auto*, *bio*, *photo*). Then move to roots that occur most often at the end of a word, or at least never occur at the *start* of a word (e.g., *-ology*, *-meter*, *-crat*, *-cracy*). Keep in mind these are suggestions only. If you're not sure where to start, these charts can help you.

Most Common Greek Roots

Root	Meaning	Sample Words
auto	self	automatic, autograph, autobiography, automobile
bio	life	biology, biosphere, biography
graph	write	graphic, geography, telegraph, photograph
hydro	water	hydrogen, hydrant, hydroplane, dehydrate
meter	measure	speedometer, odometer, thermometer, perimeter
ology	study of	geology, biology, zoology, phonology
photo	light	photograph, telephoto, photosynthesis
scope	viewing	telescope, microscope, periscope
tele	far off	telephone, telepathy, telegraph, television
therm	heat	thermos, thermometer, thermostat, thermophysics

More Greek Roots

Root	Meaning	Sample Words
phon/phono	sound	phone, phonograph, phonics
micro	small	microscope, microphone, micrometer
pol/polis	city, method of government	police, political, metropolis
crat/cracy	rule	democracy, aristocracy, democrat
geo	earth	geography, geology, geometry
metro	mother city	metropolitan, metropolis
crit	judge	critic, critical, hypocrite
path	suffer	sympathy, empathy, pathology
sphere	ball	spherical, hemisphere, atmosphere

Follow a Scope and Sequence, But Also Teach Bound Roots in Content Areas

Good word-level instruction always follows a scope and sequence. But, when appropriate, you may want to veer from your scope and sequence to teach Greek and Latin roots in their related content areas. The Greek roots can be found in technical words often used in science and math (e.g., *thermal*, *microscope*), as well as certain affixes in science (e.g., *agri-*, *cort-*, *aqua-*, *micro-*), math (e.g., *uni-*, *semi-*, *penta-*, *tri-*), and social studies (e.g., *demo-*, *hemi-*, *geo-*). When these words come up, I suggest pointing out their roots to students, and even teaching words with those roots and assessing students' knowledge of them during math, science, and social studies. For example, when doing a measurement unit during math, why not teach roots such as *centi-*, *-meter*, and *milli-*?

Ensure Latin and Greek Roots Are Taught Beyond Grade 5

Because the English language contains so many Latin and Greek roots, and because so many are used in disciplines such as science, medicine, and law, it would be unwise to try to cover all of them in elementary school! If you teach grades 4 or 5, focus on the *concept* of a bound Latin/Greek root, that the root carries the main meaning of the word, but cannot stand alone. The full inventory of Latin and Greek roots will stretch out throughout your students' educational careers.

GRADES 4 AND 5
(Very Common)

- *dict*   predict, dictate
- *auto*   automatic, autograph

MIDDLE AND HIGH SCHOOL
(More Content-Specific)

- *centi*   centigrade, centimeter
- *corpus* corporate, corporal
- *flect/x* inflexible, deflected
- *bio*   biosphere, biorhythm

COLLEGE AND CAREERS
(Less Common, Content-Specific)

- *derm*   transdermal
- *philia* hemophilia
- *opia*   myopia
- *supra* suprarenal
- *tang*   tangent

How to Teach It: Latin and Greek Roots

Although there are a few differences between Latin and Greek roots, the same basic principles apply when it comes to teaching them. Most of the activities here work for both. As with all word-level instruction, introduce roots with an explicit, systematic routine, and provide students with strategies to unpack words and understand their meanings. The activities show students how to expand roots into many different words, for example, by adding derivational (e.g., *-ion*, *-ical*, *-y*) and inflectional suffixes (e.g., *-er/est*, *-ing*).

A Routine for Teaching a Latin or Greek Root

This explicit, systematic routine begins with reminding students of how word roots work—they can't stand alone but are still the main part of the word, they must have prefixes and suffixes, they appear across many words. The routine helps students to "see the root" as a word part and internalize it.

Mesmer's Four-Step Bound Roots Routine

1 Define *root*:

"A root is the main part of a word that carries the meaning. But it cannot stand by itself. You must add prefixes and suffixes to it."

2 Introduce the root you are teaching:

"This is the Latin root *rupt-*. It is pronounced 'rupt.' It means 'to break or burst.'"

-rupt

3 Read and underline the root in words:

"Let's read some words with the root *rupt* and underline it. You will see it without prefixes and with prefixes."

rupt   <u>rupt</u>ure, inter<u>rupt</u>, e<u>rupt</u>, dis<u>rupt</u>

4 Discuss the connection between the root and the meaning of each word:

"Let's talk about each of these words and how they connect to the meaning of *-rupt*, to burst or break. So *interrupt*. The prefix *inter-* means between, or among, and *rupt* means *burst*—bursting among. *Interrupt* means bursting among. That makes sense, when people interrupt they break in among others."

Do not forget to discuss the meaning of *each* word with the root, explaining how the prefixes and suffixes build on top of the root. This last step is often forgotten, but it is essential because students do not always find the connection between the root and the word.

Peel Off Word Parts to Find the Root

Because all words with Latin and Greek roots must have some type of prefix or suffix, you can teach students to peel off the affix(es) to find the root (Lovett et al., 2000). This strategy has two purposes: to help students 1) decode the word and 2) use morphemes to understand the word. Take, for example, the word *deformed*. Students would peel off the prefix, *de-* meaning not, and the suffix *-ed*, and to reveal the root, *form*, meaning to shape. Then they would put the parts put back together and define, *deformed*: not shaped, not having a form.

Word Root Trees

Watch "Word Root Trees."

"Word Root Trees" are a great way to introduce a new word root (Bear et al., 2020). Students think about common meanings behind all the words they can find that contain a particular root (e.g., *vis*, *invisible*, *visual*, *visualize*, *envision*). Start by organizing students into small groups. Give them a large piece of chart paper, and ask them to brainstorm words with a Latin or Greek root you've chosen. Once they've assembled a list of words, have them define each one in their own words on the chart and think about the meaning of the root, based on the shared properties of the words. You might want to give students a cloze sentence to spur their thinking: "We believe the root _____ means _____ because _____." Then ask them to look up the root and correct their definition as necessary. Be sure to check each group's chart to make sure the students have the correct definition for the root and their words containing the root. Let students view each other's charts and add more words, if they can think of them.

If students do this activity in small groups, they can pool their knowledge and work together. Some teachers ask students to brainstorm across two days to give them adequate time to find lots of words. Also, they have students follow the steps described above, and then have them search for more words with the root online.

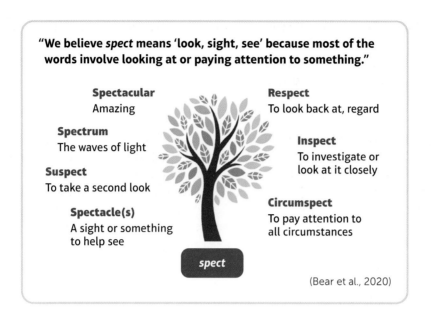

"We believe *spect* means 'look, sight, see' because most of the words involve looking at or paying attention to something."

Spectacular
Amazing

Spectrum
The waves of light

Suspect
To take a second look

Spectacle(s)
A sight or something
to help see

Respect
To look back at, regard

Inspect
To investigate or
look at it closely

Circumspect
To pay attention to
all circumstances

spect

(Bear et al., 2020)

"Word Root Trees" is an inductive activity, meaning you do not start by telling students the meaning of the root. But you should *end* the activity with an explicit, accurate definition of the word root. This approach may be more appropriate with students who are not struggling.

Given its inductive nature, this activity challenges students to analyze words; many students find it an interesting puzzle to figure out. Sometimes students identify an "imposter." For example, for the word root tree students misidentified *special*. When students identify imposters, have them examine the words, cross them out, and explain why they do not fit. This reinforces the fact that while some words contain the same letters as a root, those letters do not form a root.

Morpheme Triangles

For this activity, students start with an affixed word containing a root, take that word apart, and then generate more words that contain the prefixes, suffixes, and/ or root (Winters, 2009). By doing this, students learn how roots and other morphemes work and show up in many words. Like "Word Root Trees," I recommend having students do this activity in small groups to share knowledge and brainstorm words. However, if students know a lot about roots, they can do it independently.

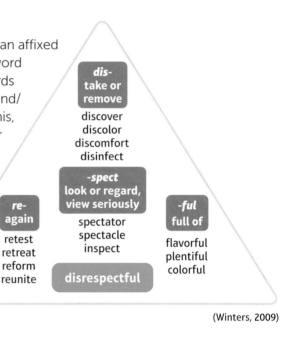

(Winters, 2009)

Latin and Greek Roots Speed Drill

Once students have learned a number of Latin and Greek roots, have them practice spotting them in different words, in various positions within those words, to recognize those words while reading. Speed drills help with that. Students underline the roots in words on a list, such as the ones shown here, practice reading each word, and then have a partner time them rereading the underlined words. This is a good activity to assign just before students read a challenging text full of words with Latin and Greek roots, or in preparation for a test.

Mix It

Watch "Mix It."

Once students have a repertoire of roots, have them combine roots with various prefixes and suffixes to create words. Start by preparing word cards in three categories: prefixes, Latin/Greek roots, and inflectional and derivational suffixes. Make sure the roots combined with the prefixes and suffixes make actual words. Then have students line up the cards with prefixes on the left, roots in the middle, and suffixes on the right. Have students leave the root in the middle and organize the prefixes to the left and suffixes to the right to create new words. They can record the words on a sheet of paper or a dry-erase board. Remind them that spelling changes may be necessary when they add certain suffixes to the root.

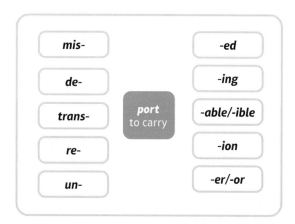

Find New and Known Roots in Content Texts

Science, math, and social studies texts are replete with words containing Latin and Greek roots, especially texts for the intermediate grades. The problem is, students will have trouble decoding those words if you have not taught their roots explicitly. Mining texts for words with roots is a perfect way to excite students! It's like sending them on a word expedition. I've found students start to show strong insights about words, whether they contain roots or not.

To prepare for this activity, choose a section from a textbook that contains words with some roots students know and others they need to learn.

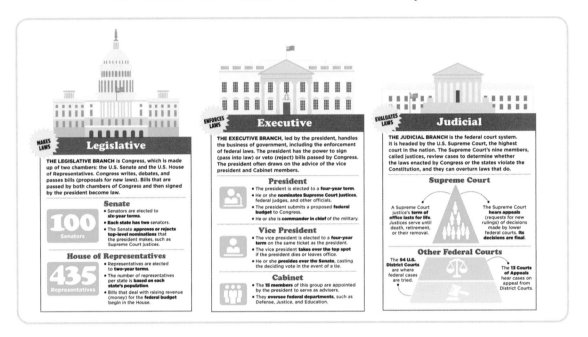

Provide students with a list of 30 or more Greek and Latin roots to use as reference as they read the section (see Appendixes F and G). First, have students look for words in the section that contain roots that they know—perhaps *judge*, *judicial* (*jud*) or *legal*, *legislation* (*leg*). Then have them look for words that they think might contain roots—perhaps *executive*, *federal*, or *constitution*. If they cannot find a root on their list, have them look up the word to determine if it is, in fact, a Greek or Latin root.

Use Cognates to Help Multilingual Learners

Cognates are words in two or more languages that have similar spellings, meanings, and sometimes pronunciations because they have similar origins. Romance languages such as English, Spanish, and French share the Latin base and contain cognates with Latin roots (e.g., *information* [English], *information* [French], *información* [Spanish], *informazione* [Italian]). During a study of Latin roots, have

Facts About Cognates

- Are words in one language that have similar spellings, meanings, and sometimes pronunciations to words in another language
- Have the same root and history

your multilingual learners show off their expertise by comparing the two words and explaining their meanings and how they are similar.

During a 15-week unit on immigration, researchers taught vocabulary to heterogeneous classes of Spanish bilinguals and English-only fifth graders (Carlo et al., 2004). Each week, they explicitly taught students 10–12 words, had students read passages containing the words, and engaged them in many activities to support word learning, including recognizing the cognates *demographics*, *debate*, and *collective*. In fact, about 68 percent of that vocabulary included cognates!

English	Spanish	Root + Affixes
information	información	*in* (with) *form* (shape)
police	policía	*pol* (city)
demographics	demografía	*dem* (people) *graph* (write)

The teachers created small groups made up of bilingual Spanish speakers and English-only speakers and asked them to identify the cognate words in passages they had read earlier in the week. The teachers identified cognates in the passages ahead of time which allowed the bilingual students to take on an expert/teacher role during the activity. After working with small groups, the teachers led the students in identifying the cognates, asking bilingual students to pronounce and explain the words. This work had strong effects on the word learning of both English-only and bilingual students.

Ongoing Anchor Charts or Notebooks

Record words on anchor charts and post those charts in a prominent place around the classroom, at students' eye level. Then throughout the year, continue to record words that contain the roots on the charts as you and your students encounter them while reading. You can also ask students to keep notebook words organized by Latin and Greek roots.

graph (hear)	*tele* (far)	*metro* (city)
telegraph	telephone	metropolis
polygraph	telegraph	metropolitan
graphic	telescope	
biography		
autograph		
photograph		

Four Ways to Help Multilingual Learners

There are specific strategies you can use to help multilingual learners. These strategies allow you to give learners extra information and support, while holding them to high standards and exposing them to robust, rich content. When teaching roots, use words in meaningful contexts and show students those words in authentic texts. At the same time, provide the words and contexts in students' first languages. If the context and/or text contains a cognate, use it! From there, show the words in other contexts so that students pick up on their connotations. For example, the word *humanity* occurs in news articles, social studies texts, and even philanthropic information.

1. Teach words using meaningful texts.	**In text:** *The many people who came to Ellis Island represented a slice of <u>humanity</u> from many places.*
2. Extend words into different contexts: a context close to the original use and one not close.	**Different context:** *It is our shared <u>humanity</u> that challenges us to help each other.*
3. Consider all facets of words to teach them (e.g., morphology, cognates, spelling, pronunciation, syntax)	Etymology: "of man" Cognate: humana/o humanidad
4. Access words and their use in texts written in students' native language and English.	*Las muchas personas que vinieron a Ellis Island representaban una porción de la <u>humanidad</u> de muchos lugares.*

(Carlo et al., 2004)

In Closing, Remember...

The upper-elementary grades are a critical time of capacity-building for reading in middle and high school. To build that capacity, instruction in word roots must be systematic and explicit. Here are a few points to remember:

- Latin and Greeks roots contain the main meaning of words, like base words, but they can't stand alone, unlike base words. They are "bound." They cannot "fly solo" and must have a prefix and/or suffix. In the upper-elementary grades, teaching Latin and Greek roots sets up this important morphological concept that will carry our students to high school graduation and into college and their careers.

- Latin and Greek roots are everywhere! Literally over 50 percent of words in advanced texts contain them. Students simply cannot do advanced reading without having access to them. And students need to be able to do more than decode roots. They must understand roots' meanings to advance their vocabulary and read widely.

- Students need explicit, systematic instruction in Latin and Greek roots so they can identify roots in words as they read. Students do not realize that roots operate within words until someone teaches them. The beauty of teaching roots is that they are so powerful, they advance students' vocabulary exponentially.

- Always follow a scope and sequence, knowing that parts of it might be best taught during science, social studies, or math (e.g., *meter*, *bio*, *geo*, *therm-*, *graph-*, *hydro*). After all, roots appear in contexts in which they are most useful.

- Students are just getting started with word roots in upper-elementary grades. They will learn dozens of roots in middle school, high school, and college. Trying to teach them all in the upper-elementary grades is a fool's errand. Teaching the most common ones, which appear on pages 129–131, is the best way to get the ball rolling.

Conclusion

Teaching pushes us toward constant cycles of improvement. There is always something to learn and always something to improve. That is the challenge. Of course, it is also the joy—that we never really arrive. There is always a new frontier, always something new to learn. If you are a teacher who has found the information in this book new, I do hope that I have pulled back the curtain to reveal new information that can improve your instruction. If you are experienced and knowledgeable in teaching big words, I hope that I have helped you gain new insights about teaching them or perhaps challenged you to see things a bit differently.

In Chapter 1, I discussed the Active View of Reading (Duke & Cartwright, 2021) and showed how understanding the parts in big words, the morphemes, bridges the connection between decoding and comprehending. When students understand the concept of a morpheme, that certain parts add meaning to words, and show up in many different words (e.g., *preseason*, *predict*, *predetermined*), then they become empowered. They can even apply that information to words they have never seen before (e.g., *preconceive*). Learning these word parts expands their abilities to read and understand exponentially! For example, if they learn just the most common inflections and derivational morphemes, they can add up to 250 additional words beyond the root words they learn. Learning word parts is like learning how to fish, instead of simply being given a fish.

Pique students' curiosity about big words. Encourage them to think about how a word works beyond phoneme-grapheme relationships. For example, in Tyler's classroom, after teaching Latin roots, he found that the students were more attuned to bound roots as they read. "It was the weirdest thing, I only taught the most common ones like *vis*, *cred*, *struct*, but after I did that,

I found that they would pick up on ones while they read and would bring them to me. The other day, Pardeep spotted the word *leg* in *legislate* and made the connection between *legal* and *legislate*." I also find that teachers themselves become curious and report turning to online dictionaries and resources to learn more about the parts in words they read. Of course, this further drives a spirit of inquiry and excitement in the classroom.

We simply can't wait until third grade to teach big words. We can start building the foundation for the morphological elements of English right away. I like to think of big-words instruction as learning "word architecture" or design. Phoneme-grapheme relationships are like bricks and mortar but morphemes are walls and rooms. It makes absolutely no sense to give kids bricks and mortar and not tell them the design of words. My hope is that this book will help you begin that journey for yourself.

APPENDIX A: Decodable Compound Words Grouped by Pattern

CVC Pattern	Blends	Digraphs and Blends	Vowel Teams and r-Controlled Words		
bed bedbug bedroll bedsit	**hand** handbag handcuff handset	**back** backbend backchat backdrop backend backfill backflip backhand backlash backless backlog backlot backpack backrest backslap backslid backspin backstab backstop backtrack	**air** aircraft airfield airlift airport air + silent *e* airtime airline airplane	**life** lifeblood lifeboat lifeguard lifelong life + silent *e* lifelike lifeline lifetime	**watch** watchband watchdog watchman watchword
	crosscut		**ball** ballpark ballroom	**main** mainland mainline	**week** weekday weekend weeknight
cat catgut catnap catnip	hotspot	**black** blacklist blacktop blacktip blacksmith	back + silent *e* backbite backbone backside backslide backspace backstage backstroke backfire background	**moon** moonbeam moonlight moonshine moonstruck	
hilltop	himself	catfish	baseball	nearby	
				night nightclub nightdress nightgown nightstand overnight weeknight	
hot hotbed hotbox hotcake hotdog	**in** inbred inland inset	**dish** dishcloth dishpan dishrag	**bed** bedclothes bedroom	northeast	

Go to scholastic.com/bigwordsresources for a downloadable version of this list (Source: Spelfabet.com).

BIG WORDS FOR YOUNG READERS

CVC Pattern	Blends	Digraphs and Blends	Vowel Teams and r-Controlled Words	
offset	itself	**fish** fishnet fishpond	**black** blackball blackbird blackboard blackmail blackout	**news** newsboy newsbreak newsprint newsreel newsroom newsstand
red redcap redfin	**sand** sandbox sandlot	**flat** flatbed flatpack flattop	**blue** bluebell bluebird bluefish bluegrass blueprint	nowhere
setup	**sun** Sunbelt sunlamp sunspot	**strong** strongbox stronghold strongman	**book** bookcase bookend bookmark bookshelf bookstore bookworm	**pin** pinhole pinstripe pinwheel
sun sunbed sunhat sunlit sunset suntan sunup	**stand** standoff standout	**pot** potluck potshot	cardboard	pancake
up upend uphill upon upset	**up** upheld uplift	**stick** stickman stickpin stickup	**book** bookcase bookend bookmark bookshelf bookstore bookworm	playhouse
		sun sundeck sunfish	**day** daybreak daydream daylight daytime	popcorn
		grand grandchild granddad grandmom		**rain** rainbow raincheck raincoat raindrop rainstorm
		hotshot	caveman	**school** schoolbook schoolboy schoolhouse schoolwork
		jackpot	cheesecake	railway

Go to scholastic.com/bigwordsresources for a downloadable version of this list (Source: Spelfabet.com).

CVC Pattern	Blends	Digraphs and Blends	Vowel Teams and r-Controlled Words		
		matchbox	comeback	seashore	
		pickup	cornmeal	sheepskin	
		setback	deadline	shoelace	
			downbeat	shortbread	
			drawbridge	showoff	
			earth earthquake earthworm	**side** sideburns sidekick sidewalk	
			eye eyeball eyelash eyelid eyesight	skateboard	
			fire firearm fireball firebomb firebreak fireflies fireproof fireworks	**snow** snowball snowbank snowbird snowdrift	
			fish fishbowl fishhook fishtail	**soft** softball software	
			foot football foothill footlights footnote footprints footrest	**some** someday somehow someone someplace	
			forklift	**south** southeast southwest	
			friendship	**stand** standby standout standpoint	
			goodbye	starfish	
			gumball	steamboat steamship	

BIG WORDS FOR YOUNG READERS

CVC Pattern	Blends	Digraphs and Blends	Vowel Teams and *r*-Controlled Words		
			hand handbook handmade handout	**sun** sunbaked sunbathe sundown sunroof	
			head headdress headlight headline headstone	**tail** tailgate taillight tailspin	
			herself	**take** takeoff takeout	
			high highchair highway	**tea** teacup teapot teaspoon	
			home homemade hometown	teamwork	
			horse horsefly horsehair horseplay	**tooth** toothpaste toothpick	
			house houseboat household	touchdown	
			in inside intake	**up** upbeat update upgrade upkeep upload upright uproar uproot upstage upstairs upstart upstream uptight	
			key keyboard keynote keypad keystroke	**wash** washcloth washout washroom washstand	

Go to scholastic.com/bigwordsresources for a downloadable version of this list (Source: Spelfabet.com).

APPENDIX B: Lists for Make It Big

The "Make It Big" activity described on page 76 in Chapter 5 is great for K–1, when students are working on inflections that do not require a spelling change to the base word. Start by finding a pattern on this list that you have taught (e.g., -st), and select the base word (dust). From there, set up inflections that work with it (e.g., -er, -s, -ing) and compound words that combine with it (e.g., bin, men, up > dustbin, dustmen, dustup) as in the picture.

Note: An "x" under an inflection indicates that the base word requires a spelling change (e.g., fish > fishes). Do not give students that inflection as an option unless you've taught them the spelling change.

Pattern	Base	-s	-er	-ing	-ed	Compounds
-sh	fish	x	fisher	fishing	fished	fishnet, fishpond, catfish, sunfish
-nch	bench	x	x	benching	benched	workbench, backbench, benchmark
-tch	watch	x	watcher	watching	watched	watchband, watchdog, watchman
-ck	back	backs	backer	backing	backed	backpack, backbend, backdrop, backflip
-ck	stick	sticks	sticker	sticking	x	stick, stickman, stickpin, stickup
-ck	rock	rocks	rocker	rocking	rocked	bedrock, rockfall
-st	dust	dusts	duster	dusting	dusted	dustbin, dustmen, dustup
-nd	sand	sands	sander	sanding	sanded	sandlot, sandbox, sandbag
-mp	camp	camps	camper	camping	camped	campsite, campground, camp
ay	play	plays	player	playing	played	playset, playpen
ai	rail	rails	x	railing	railed	railroad, railyard, railcar
ai	rain	rains	x	raining	rained	raincoat, rainbow, rainstorm, raindrop
ai	sail	sails	x	sailing	sailed	sailboat, sailfish, sailcloth, topsail
ea	team	teams	x	teaming	teamed	teamwork, teammate, team
ee	sleep	sleeps	sleeper	sleeping	x	sleepwalk, sleepshirt, sleepover
oa	boat	boats	boater	boating	boated	steamboat, houseboat, lifeboat
ow	snow	snows	x	snowing	snowed	snowball, snowbank, snowdrift, snowflake
oo	room	rooms	x	rooming	roomed	roommate, bedroom, bathroom, washroom, ballroom
ew	view	views	viewer	viewing	viewed	overview, viewpoint, worldview
igh	fight	fights	fighter	fighting	x	catfight, dogfight, firefight, fistfight

Go to scholastic.com/bigwordsresources for a downloadable version of this list.

APPENDIX C: Two- and Three-Syllable Words by Syllable Type

1. Closed Syllable

catnip	lipstick	cotton	gossip	sudden	cutback	submit
lunchbox	sandbox	traffic	litter	happen	pumpkin	backpack
sunset	button	kitten	butter	basket	uplift	
pigpen	mitten	rotten	rabbit	plastic	unzip	

2. Open Syllable

hotel	began	hero	final	bacon	pilot	tulip
silo	program	evil	robot	halo	tidal	
music	zero	zebra	basin	bison	vital	

3. Silent e

grapevine	lifeline	stovepipe	homeplace	racetrack
whalebone	baseball	homemade	pinhole	smokestack
sunrise	pancake	nosedive	milestone	placemat

4. Vowel Teams

beekeeper	snowflake	toenail	reason	complain	indeed
window	snowman	peanut	oatmeal	bobtail	explain
boatload	railroad	leaflet	soapbox	sixteen	balloon
maintain	cookbook	teapot	contain	coffee	

5. r-Controlled

partner	carpet	target	perform	father	collar	charter
unicorn	garden	water	corner	harbor	bitter	harder
farmer	marvel	former	mother	barber	doctor	

6. Consonant -le

sniffle	waffle	paddle	startle	noodle	giggle	fizzle
ruffle	raffle	candle	fable	eagle	bugle	
snuffle	battle	gentle	stable	able	puzzle	
jiggle	bottle	purple	rifle	title	sizzle	
cattle	tattle	gargle	noble	juggle	nozzle	

Go to scholastic.com/bigwordsresources for a downloadable version of this list.

APPENDIX D: Prefixes

Prefix	Meaning	Sample Words
The Most Frequent Prefixes (in 75 percent of words with prefixes)		
un-	not	unwrap, unfreeze, undo, unable
re-	again	rewrap, rewrite, redo, reconsider, replay
in-/im-/il-/ir-	not	immortal, illegible, illegal, impossible, insecure
dis-	opposite	disrupt, dispel, distract, dismiss
en-/em-	cause to be	embolden, embed, encourage, empower
non-	not	nonstop, nonstick, nonfiction, nonverbal
in-	in	inspect, intend, invent
over-	over	overlook, overdo, overcook, overheat
mis-	wrong	mistake, misinterpret, misspell
More Prefixes		
sub-	under	subway, subscript, submarine, subgroup
pre-	before	preform, prescription, prewrite, pretest
inter-	between	interstate, interjection, interference, internet
fore-	before	before, foreground, foretell, foreshadow
de-	away from, off	defrost, degrade, deflate, deice, decompose
trans-	across	transport, transatlantic, transfer, transit
super-	over, big	superimpose, superficial, superscript, superhighway
semi-	half, past	semicircle, semifinal, semiannual
mid-	middle	midlevel, midweek, midterm, midwife
under-	under	undergo, underplay, underpin, underwear
anti-	against	anticlimax, antifreeze, antiseptic, antibacterial
bi-	two	bicycle, bisect, bicep, biannual
cent-	100	century, centennial, centimeter
circum-	around, circle	circumference, circumspect, circumflex

Go to scholastic.com/bigwordsresources for a downloadable version of this list.

BIG WORDS FOR YOUNG READERS

Prefix	Meaning	Sample Words
co-	with, together	coexist, cooperate, cohort, coauthor
con-		construct, connect, concert, condense
com-		communicate, common, community, complete
ex-	without	exclaim, exile, exhaust, extract, exceed
mill-	million	millimeter, millipede, millennium
multi-	many	multitude, multiple, multiply, multimedia
mono-/mon-	one, only	monarchy, monopoly, monorail, monogram
oct-	eight	octagon, octagonal, October
pro-	forward, before	proclaim, profile, propel, profess, produce
peri-	around	period, perimeter, periphery
poly-	many	polygon, polymer, polytechnic, polyp
post-	after	posterior, postpone, postgame, postscript
semi-	half	semicircle, semiannual, semifinal, semicolon
tri-	three	tricycle, triangle, triangular
uni-	one, only	universe, uniform, unity, unique

(Eide, 2012)

Go to scholastic.com/bigwordsresources for a downloadable version of this list.

APPENDIX E: Suffixes (Inflectional and Derivational)

Suffix	Meaning	Sample Words
The Most Frequent Suffixes		
-s/-es*	inflection plural or verb tense	puppies, bunches, horses, dogs runs, brushes, tries
-ed*	inflection past tense	coated, liked, bagged
-ing*	inflection participle	hoping, leaping, popping
-ly	adverb making	happily, gladly, sadly
-er	noun making "one who"	runner, packer, diver Note: -er is also a derivational suffix
-ion/-tion/-ation/-ition	noun making "act or process of"	action, creation, repetition, possession
-able/-ible	adjective making "being able to"	visible, breakable, changeable, credible
-al/-ial	adjective making "having characteristics of"	accidental, historical, tribal, territorial
-y	adjective making "characterized by"	grumpy, weepy, jumpy
-ness	noun making "state of being"	laziness, happiness, quickness
More Suffixes		
-ity/-ty	noun making "quality of"	equity, ability, unity, activity
-ment	noun making "condition of"	commitment, excitement, requirement
-ic/-ical	adjective making "characteristic of"	electric, political, magical, critical
-ous/-eous	adjective making "full of"	zealous, perilous, boisterous, nauseous
-en	adjective making "full of, made of"	waxen, wooden, golden
-er*	inflection comparative	big, bigger

Go to scholastic.com/bigwordsresources for a downloadable version of this list.

BIG WORDS FOR YOUNG READERS

Suffix	Meaning	Sample Words
-ive, -ative, -tive	adjective making "tendency"	destructive, constructive, reactive
-ful	adjective making "full of"	beautiful, plentiful, tearful
-less	adjective making "less"	boundless, limitless, smokeless
-est*	inflection superlative	red, reddest
More Derivational Suffixes		
-acy	noun making "state or quality of"	privacy, advocacy, accuracy
-ance/-ence	noun making "state or quality of"	existence, defiance, independence, evidence
-ate	verb making "to become"	differentiate, activate, negotiate
-ify, -fy	verb making "make or become"	beautify, amplify, clarify
-ize/-ise	verb making "become"	specialize, prioritize, categorize
-hood	noun making "state of being"	statehood, neighborhood, nationhood
-ism	noun making "belief or doctrine"	capitalism, communism, socialism
-ist	noun making "one who"	chemist, pharmacist, artist, harpist
-or	noun making "one who"	actor, doctor
-ology	noun making "study of"	biology, geology, gerontology

Note: Shaded suffixes are inflections (Eide, 2012).

Go to scholastic.com/bigwordsresources for a downloadable version of this list.

APPENDIX F: Latin Roots

Root	Meaning	Sample Words
Most Common Latin Roots		
aud	hear	audience, auditory, auditorium, audible
dict	speak, say	dictate, predict, dictation, edict
ject	throw	eject, reject, subject, project
port	carry	transport, portable, report, porter
rupt	break	erupt, rupture, disrupt, interrupt
scrib/script	write	scribe, scripture, scribble, prescribe, describe
spect	look	inspect, spectate, respect
struct	build	construct, reconstruct, structure, instruct
tract	pull	tractor, traction, detract, extract
vis	see	visual, vision, supervise, visualize
More Latin Roots		
cred	believe	credible, incredible, credit, credibility, discredit
duct/duce	lead	reduce, produce, induce, conduct
equa/equi	equal	equity, equitable, inequitable, equality, inequality
flect/flex	bend	reflex, flexible, deflect, inflect
form	shape	deform, formation, formative, inform, reform, uniform
grac/grat	thank	gracious, grateful, gratitude, gratuity
sequ/sec	follow	sequel, sequence, sequential
vac	empty	vacuum, vacant, vacate, vacation
voc	call	vocal, vocation, invoke, revoke

Go to scholastic.com/bigwordsresources for a downloadable version of this list.

BIG WORDS FOR YOUNG READERS

APPENDIX G: Greek Roots

Root	Meaning	Sample Words
Most Common Greek Roots		
auto	self	automatic, autograph, autobiography, automobile
bio	life	biology, biosphere, biography
graph	write	graphic, geography, telegraph, photograph
hydro	water	hydrogen, hydrant, hydroplane, dehydrate
meter	measure	speedometer, odometer, thermometer, perimeter
ology	study of	geology, biology, zoology, phonology
photo	light	photograph, telephoto, photosynthesis
scope	viewing instrument	telescope, microscope, periscope
tele	far off	telephone, telepathy, telegraph, television
therm	heat	thermos, thermometer, thermostat, thermophysics
More Greek Roots		
arch	chief	architecture, monarch, hierarchy
centr	center	central, concentrate
chron	time	chronicle, chronology, chronic
cycl	circle	cycle, cyclical, bicycle, recycle
dem	people	democracy, democrat, demagogue
dys	bad, hard	dysfunction, dyslexia
gram	to write	telegram, grammar, diagram, program
logo	word or reason	logic, logistics, logical, dialogue
phil	love	philosophy, philanthropy, hydrophilic
phobia	fear	phobic, hydrophobic
psych	soul, spirit	psychology, psychic, psychological
pseudo	false	pseudonym, pseudoscience
phys	nature	physical, physics, physician
tech	skill, art	technician, technical, technique

Go to scholastic.com/bigwordsresources for a downloadable version of this list.

References

Anglin, J. M., Miller, G. A., & Wakefield, P. C. (1993). Vocabulary development: A morphological analysis. *Monographs of the Society for Research in Child Development*, i–186.

Balota, D. A., Yap, M. J., Hutchison, K. A., Cortese, M. J., Kessler, B., Loftis, B., ... Treiman, R. (2007). The English lexicon project. *Behavior Research Methods, 39*, 445–459.

Baumann, J. F., Edwards, E. C., Boland, E. M., Olejnik, S., & Kame'enui, E. J. (2003). Vocabulary tricks: Effects of instruction in morphology and context on fifth-grade students' ability to derive and infer word meanings. *American Educational Research Journal, 40*(2), 447–494.

Bear, D. R., Invernizzi, M., Templeton, S., & Johnston, F. R. (2020). *Words their way: Word study for phonics, vocabulary, and spelling instruction*. Pearson Higher Ed.

Beck, I. L., & Beck, M. E. (2013). *Making sense of phonics: The hows and whys*. The Guilford Press.

Berninger, V. W., Abbott, R., Nagy, W., & Carlisle, J. (2010). Growth in phonological, orthographic, and morphological awareness in grades 1 to 6. *Journal of Psycholinguistic Research, 39*, 141–163.

Bhattacharya, A., & Ehri, L. C. (2004). Graphosyllabic analysis helps adolescent struggling readers read and spell words. *Journal of Learning Disabilities, 37*(4), 331–348.

Blevins, W. (2023). *Phonics from A to Z: A practical guide* (4th ed.). Scholastic.

Blevins, W. (2023). *Teaching phonics & word study in the intermediate grades: A complete sourcebook*. Scholastic.

Bowers, P. N., Kirby, J. R., & Deacon, S. H. (2010). The effects of morphological instruction on literacy skills: A systematic review of the literature. *Review of Educational Research, 80*(2), 144–179.

Carlisle, J. F. (2000). Awareness of the structure and meaning of morphologically complex words: Impact on reading. *Reading and Writing, 12*, 169–190.

Carlo, M. S., August, D., McLaughlin, B., Snow, C. E., Dressler, C., Lippman, D. N., Lively, T. J., & White, C. E. (2004). Closing the gap: Addressing the vocabulary needs of English-language learners in bilingual and mainstream classrooms. *Reading Research Quarterly, 39*(2), 188–215.

Carroll, J. B., Davies, P., & Richman, B. (1971). *The American heritage word frequency book*. Houghton Mifflin.

Chomsky, C. (1970). Reading, writing, and phonology. *Harvard Educational Review, 40*(2), 287–309.

Cunningham, A. E., Firestone, A. R., & Zegers, M. (2023). Measuring and improving teachers' knowledge in early literacy. In S. Q. Cabell, S. B. Neuman, and N. Patton Terry (Eds.), *Handbook on the science of early literacy* (p. 211). Guildford Press.

Derwing, B. L. (1976). Morpheme recognition and the learning of rules for derivational morphology. *Canadian Journal of Linguistics/Revue canadienne de linguistique, 21*(1), 38–66.

Duke, N. K., & Cartwright, K. B. (2021). The science of reading progresses: Communicating advances beyond the simple view of reading. *Reading Research Quarterly, 56*, S25–S44.

Ehri, L. C. (2005). Learning to read words: Theory, findings, and issues. *Scientific Studies of Reading, 9*(2), 167–188.

Eide, D. (2012). *Uncovering the logic of English: A commonsense solution to America's literacy crisis*. Logic of English, Inc.

Eldredge, J. L. (2005). *Teaching decoding: Why and how*. Merrill, Prentice-Hall.

Espinosa, C. M., & Ascenzi-Moreno, L. (2021). *Rooted in strength: Using translanguaging to grow multilingual readers and writers*. Scholastic.

Ganske, K. (2020). *Mindful of words: Spelling and vocabulary explorations, grades 4–8*. The Guilford Press.

Gates, L., & Yale, I. (2011). A logical letter-sound system in five phonic generalizations. *The Reading Teacher, 64*(5), 330–339.

Goodwin, A. P., & Ahn, S. (2013). A meta-analysis of morphological interventions in English: Effects on literacy outcomes for school-age children. *Scientific Studies of Reading, 17*(4), 257–285.

Goodwin, A. P., Gilbert, J. K., & Cho, S. J. (2013). Morphological contributions to adolescent word reading: An item response approach. *Reading Research Quarterly, 48*(1), 39–60.

Goodwin, A. P., Gilbert, J. K., Cho, S. J., & Kearns, D. M. (2014). Probing lexical representations: Simultaneous modeling of word and reader contributions to multidimensional lexical representations. *Journal of Educational Psychology, 106*(2), 448.

Goodwin, A. P., Lipsky, M., & Ahn, S. (2012). Word detectives: Using units of meaning to support literacy. *The Reading Teacher, 65*(7), 461–470.

Goodwin, A. P., Petscher, Y., Jones, S., McFadden, S., Reynolds, D., & Lantos, T. (2020). The monster in the classroom: Assessing language to inform instruction. *The Reading Teacher, 73*(5), 603–616.

Goodwin, A. P., Petscher, Y., & Tock, J. (2021). Multidimensional morphological assessment for middle school students. *Journal of Research in Reading, 44*(1), 70–89.

Gough, P. B., & Tunmer, W. E. (1986). Decoding, reading, and reading disability. *Remedial and Special Education, 7*(1), 6–10.

Helman, L. A., Bear, D. R., Templeton, S., Invernizzi, M., & Johnston, F. (2012). *Words their way with English learners: Word study for phonics, vocabulary, and spelling*. Pearson.

Henry, M. K. (2010). *Words: Integrated decoding and spelling instruction based on word origin and word structure* (2nd ed.). ProEd.

Henry, M. K. (2019). Morphemes matter: A framework for instruction. *Perspectives on Language and Literacy, 45*(2), 23–26.

Hoover, W. A., & Gough, P. B. (1990). The simple view of reading. *Reading and Writing, 2*, 127–160.

Hoover, W. A., & Tunmer, W. E. (2018). The simple view of reading: Three assessments of its adequacy. *Remedial and Special Education, 39*(5), 304–312.

Hoover, W. A., & Tunmer, W. E. (2020). *The cognitive foundations of reading and its acquisition*. Springer.

Jones, A. C., Wardlow, L., Pan, S. C., Zepeda, C., Heyman, G. D., Dunlosky, J., & Rickard, T. C. (2016). Beyond the rainbow: Retrieval practice leads to better spelling than does rainbow writing. *Educational Psychology Review, 28*, 385–400.

Jump, J., & Johnson, R. D. (2022). *What the science of reading says about word recognition*. Teacher-Created Materials.

Kearns, D. M., & Hiebert, E. H. (2022). The word complexity of primary-level texts: Differences between first and third grade in widely used curricula. *Reading Research Quarterly, 57*(1), 255–285.

Kieffer, M. J., & Lesaux, N. K. (2007). Breaking down words to build meaning: Morphology, vocabulary, and reading comprehension in the urban classroom. *The Reading Teacher, 61*(2), 134–144.

Knight-McKenna, M. (2008). Syllable types: A strategy for reading multisyllabic words. *Teaching Exceptional Children, 40*(3), 18.

Kuhn, M. R., & Stahl, K. A. D. (2022). Teaching reading: Development and differentiation. *Phi Delta Kappan, 103*(8), 25–31.

Lovett, M. W., Lacerenza, L., & Borden, S. L. (2000). Putting struggling readers on the PHAST track: A program to integrate phonological and strategy-based remedial reading instruction and maximize outcomes. *Journal of Learning Disabilities, 33*(5), 458–476.

Lovett, M. W., Lacerenza, L., Borden, S. L., Frijters, J. C., Steinbach, K. A., & De Palma, M. (2000). Components of effective remediation for developmental reading disabilities: Combining phonological and strategy-based instruction to improve outcomes. *Journal of Educational Psychology, 92*(2), 263.

Manyak, P. C., Baumann, J. F., & Manyak, A. M. (2018). Morphological analysis instruction in the elementary grades: Which morphemes to teach and how to teach them. *The Reading Teacher, 72*(3), 289–300.

Moats, L. C., & Brady, S. (2000). *Speech to print: Language essentials for teachers*. Paul H. Brookes Publisher.

Moats, L. C., & Tolman, C. A. (2019). *Language essentials for teachers of reading and spelling*. Sopris.

Nagy, W. E., & Anderson, R. C. (1984). How many words are there in printed school English? *Reading Research Quarterly*, 304–330.

Nation, K. (2019). Children's reading difficulties, language, and reflections on the simple view of reading. *Australian Journal of Learning Difficulties, 24*(1), 47–73.

Park, Y., Benedict, A. E., & Brownell, M. T. (2014). Construct and predictive validity of the CORE Phonics Survey: A diagnostic assessment for students with specific learning disabilities. *Exceptionality, 22*(1), 33.

Powell, D. A., & Aram, R. (2008). Spelling in parts: A strategy for spelling and decoding polysyllabic words. *The Reading Teacher, 61*(7), 567–570.

Scarborough, H. (2001). Connecting early language and literacy to later reading (dis)abilities: evidence, theory, and practice. In S. B. Neuman & D. K. Dickinson (Eds.), *Handbook of early literacy research* (Vol. 1, pp. 97–110). The Guilford Press.

Scarborough, H. S., Neuman, S., & Dickinson, D. (2009). Connecting early language and literacy to later reading (dis)abilities: Evidence, theory, and practice. *Approaching Difficulties in Literacy Development: Assessment, Pedagogy and Programmes, 10*, 23–38.

Shefelbine, J. (1990). A syllabic-unit approach to teaching decoding of polysyllabic words to fourth- and sixth-grade disabled readers. *National Reading Conference Yearbook, 39*, 223–229.

Tortorelli, L. S., Lupo, S. M., & Wheatley, B. C. (2021). Examining teacher preparation for code-related reading instruction: An integrated literature review. *Reading Research Quarterly, 56*, S317–S337.

Toste, J. R., Capin, P., Williams, K. J., Cho, E., & Vaughn, S. (2019). Replication of an experimental study investigating the efficacy of a multisyllabic word reading intervention with and without motivational beliefs training for struggling readers. *Journal of Learning Disabilities, 52*(1), 45–58.

Toste, J. R., Williams, K. J., & Capin, P. (2017). Reading big words: Instructional practices to promote multisyllabic word reading fluency. *Intervention in School and Clinic, 52*(5), 270–278.

Tyler, A., & Nagy, W. (1989). The acquisition of English derivational morphology. *Journal of Memory and Language, 28*(6), 649–667.

Valdez-Pierce, L. (2023). *The assessment of English language learners*. https://www.readingrockets.org/helping-all-readers/voices-experts/webcasts/assessment-english-language-learners

Walpole, S., McKenna, M. C., Philippakos, Z. A., & Strong, J. Z. (2019). *Differentiated literacy instruction in grades 4 and 5: Strategies and resources*. The Guilford Press.

Willingham, D. T. (2017). *The reading mind: A cognitive approach to understanding how the mind reads*. John Wiley & Sons.

Wheeler, R., Cartwright, K. B., & Swords, R. (2012). Factoring AAVE into reading assessment and instruction. *The Reading Teacher, 65*(6), 416–425.

Wheeler, R., & Swords, R. S. (2015). *Code-switching lessons: Grammar strategies for linguistically diverse writers*. Ventris Learning.

Winters, R. (2009). Interactive frames for vocabulary growth and word consciousness. *The Reading Teacher, 62*(8), 685–690.

Index